To Aan & Brian
Health Wealth + Happiness
Always

Feng Shui
for You

Feng Shui For You

Published by:
Greatest Guides Limited, Woodstock, Bridge End, Warwick
CV34 6PD, United Kingdom

www.greatestguides.com

Greatest Guides is committed to a sustainable future for our
planet. This book is printed on paper certified by the Forest
Stewardship Council.

Printed and bound in the United Kingdom

ISBN 978-1-907906-18-3

To my son Robi

Your transformation is my inspiration!

Contents

A few words from Suzanne …

One of the key questions that needs answering on our planet today is how we create harmony, so that as people of different races, colors and creeds, we can live together peacefully. On a micro level, it would seem that one of the best places to start solving this problem is in our own homes and offices in our daily lives right now.

I have been attracted to the study of balance and harmony within the individual on many levels, physically, mentally, emotionally and spiritually.

One of the things I most like about feng shui is, that whatever anyone's circumstances, whether you live in a tent, an apartment, a mansion or a palace, the same basic principles apply. The sense of harmony that results from their careful and loving application is an ongoing delight.

This book is written so that you can dip in to and out of it – not necessarily in sequence, though I do recommend reading Chapter 2 – 'Getting Started' first.

You may find repetitions and reminders about the more important information. This is done deliberately to ensure that you overlook nothing, and get the most out of the material, which is intended to be a very practical guide.

Feng shui is really about your interaction with your personal space. We often forget that we are territorial creatures. For our ancestors, spatial awareness, and who and what was around them was, very frequently, a matter of life and death.

While the way we live life at the minute may not be so dramatic, our 'territory' and whatever happens on it and in it, still remains hugely relevant and important to us.

Big thank yous!

To

All the sages, scribes and translators of the I Ching, whose words echo down the corridors of time.

All the feng shui masters and teachers, past and present, whose contributions keep this subject alive.

William Spear, my first teacher, for his inspirational translation of Eastern wisdom into practical Western ways.

Everyone who has contributed, directly and indirectly to the making of this book, and especially to my wonderful PA, Sacha Bond, for her patience and attention to detail.

And most of all, to you, the reader, for your time and curiosity as you explore the contribution that feng shui can make to your life.

May it far exceed your expectations and bring you ongoing delight.

Dr Suzanne G Harper
Premier House
10 Greycoat Place
LONDON
SW1P 1SB

What Is Feng Shui?

" We cannot direct the wind, but we can adjust the sails. "

Dolly Parton

Chapter 1
What Is Feng Shui?

When people talk about feng shui they often think that it just means moving their furniture around. If only it were that simple!

Feng shui is about organizing space and time in relation to individuals and groups of people to create balance and harmony. The rules that it uses are very ancient ones, based on Taoist philosophy.

This way of looking at the world is also at the root of traditional acupuncture. It takes into account the seasons, and the cycles of the earth – Sun and Moon, day and night. It's also about Yin and Yang – the balance of elements as explained in the I Ching, the 5,000 year old Chinese book of wisdom and the duality of life.

On the face of it, we 21st century humans are living very differently from our ancestors. (However, for "duality" read "binary system", which is what all our computer technology is based around and perhaps we are not so different after all.)

Originally, feng shui was the preserve of emperors in ancient China. It was considered so powerful that it was customary for the feng shui master to be restricted to the emperor's palace and grounds.

3,000 thousand years ago, only men were feng shui masters, and the art was passed down from father to son. Fortunately, things have moved on and nowadays women, as well as men, practice this fascinating art.

Businesses in both the East and West use feng shui to increase their profits as well as improving working conditions for their staff and, most important of all, attracting customers.

DO PEOPLE REALLY GET A NEW LIFE BY MOVING THEIR FURNITURE AROUND?

Have you ever considered that every supposedly inanimate object in your home, or your office, is a symbol that has its own psychological significance for you? It also relates to one of 8 types of energy, as well as 1 of the 5 basic elements, of Chinese medicine?

When you move your furniture around, you are changing the inter-relationship of different symbols, and the way that they relate to you as well as to each other. It is about much more than just the layout of your living room!

There are many people in the East, especially in Japan, who notice space first and the objects in the space second. A classic example of this is the following illustration.

What do you see? Do you see an old woman with a scarf or a young woman with a necklace? Of course both images are present simultaneously.

As the placement of the objects in your home changes, your relationship with what they symbolize also changes. Location, location and more location describes the power of claiming any space you use as your own, and occupying it consciously.

WHAT SORT OF RESULTS CAN I EXPECT?

Expect the unexpected! You may find that events work out in your favor, but not in the way you expected. Frequently, when you have given up altogether, something wonderful happens.

For example, it is not uncommon for clients to find their ideal job through word of mouth, or recommendation from a friend, despite having sent out over 70 résumés, and being on the books of over 5 agents. In some cases, the job stays the same, but the rewards escalate, as the following real life example illustrates.

A friend of mine, who was looking for more work, made the feng shui changes in his home.

He and his wife had been planning a house move as well. This would have entailed his wife giving up her existing job. The wife's employer, on discovering that she was about to quit, immediately doubled her salary, and asked her if she would be willing to stay.

After talking it over with her husband, they decided that, as this would raise the family income beyond the level they had expected, they did not need to move.

He, subsequently, found other work as well. It was a win-win situation all round. It certainly did not happen according to plan. What is even more interesting is that this gentleman's wife, up until that time, had no interest or belief in feng shui whatsoever!

HOW DO YOU KNOW WHEN IT IS WORKING?

You know that the feng shui of your home or your office is really on track when the right people and the right things just seem to show up out of nowhere at the right time. In a word, it is very positive synchronicity.

WHAT DOES IT NOT INFLUENCE?

Feng shui influences your luck. It does not change your destiny, although some Eastern thinkers consider that it may mitigate your karma.

WHAT IS DESTINY?

Matters of survival, life, death and birth all relate to destiny.

Doing feng shui in your home can help you conceive, so that you find, or stumble upon, all the necessary help. However, this is considered to be a matter of destiny.

In other words, if you are destined to have 1 child or 3 children, you will anyway.

It may be that you, or your spouse, are sleeping over geopathic stress or vortex energy. You move your bed off this area. Your health subsequently improves. Hey presto, you are pregnant!

Maybe you have missing space in the North of your home. You correct it, and you conceive shortly thereafter.

It may be that when you emphasize the '**Offspring**' area of your home with heavy furniture, and a mirror reflecting family art work, you become pregnant naturally, despite having failed with IVF.

All of these scenarios have actually happened for clients of mine. However, as this relates to destiny, it is to be hoped for, rather than expected.

Likewise, your children each have their own destinies. If you have an artistic child, and try to push him or her into being a lawyer, feng shui will not help you do this.

Also, doing feng shui in your home will not prevent anyone close to you from dying. I have had clients complain to me about deaths in their family, and have pointed out that matters of life and death are beyond the remit of feng shui.

When you share a household with other people, your own bedroom is at least 70% of your feng shui, so don't worry that your housemate's messy habits are ruining your good luck! That is their problem. In feng shui terms, it is your personal space that is important.

Relating to your love life, if your present partner is part of your destiny, feng shui will bring you closer together. If this is not the case, you will find that doing feng shui in your space will make this apparent. Fortunately, what usually happens in these circumstances is that the split is as amicable, and peaceful as possible.

It is impossible for any consultant to know in advance which way things will go.

I have turned up to do a consultation when one partner was literally packing his bags. The couple decided to go through with the consultation anyway, and subsequently stayed together.

I have also gone to other homes where, despite doing all the necessary feng shui changes, it has become apparent that both partners' lives are taking them in completely different directions, and for each of them to fulfil their purpose, they need to be apart.

TIMING

The Past

In the East, in terms of good luck, good karma and good fortune, you are considered 'dead in the water' if you do not take care of your ancestors. In Eastern terms, this translates into the up-keep of your ancestors' graves and visiting these burial grounds from time to time.

In the West, and given that many families are scattered over the globe, it is perhaps more relevant for us to mark the anniversary of a relative's passing in some other way.

It is quite common for people to dream of a dead relative or friend around the time of year that they died. Some people find this physically and emotionally disturbing, until they remember that this time is the anniversary of the passing of a loved one.

Once they realize this and, either say a prayer or mark the date in some way, a sense of peace returns.

An attitude of gratitude to those who have gone before us is also extremely helpful. Most parents and families strive to enable the new generations that follow them to go on to better things.

The Present

Feng shui relates to both time and space. Expect to make yearly adjustments in order to continue to get positive results.

Be aware that 1 year out of every 9, mirrors and red objects need to be moved, or specific adjustments made for their presence.

Failure to do this results in outside interference in your plans. It may take several years, especially for a business, to re-balance the consequences.

The Future

As your life changes, your priorities change and it is important to adjust your space accordingly to reflect your new situation. This is especially relevant in terms of:

A lover moving in with you
An elderly parent coming to live with you
A new baby as well as, of course,
Moving house and/or business premises (even if you are employed)

Please see Chapter 9 for more information on all these situations.

DO I NEED TO BE A HOMEOWNER FOR IT TO WORK?

Feng shui relates to your own personal space. This is true whether you are a:

- Teenager living at home

- Single person living in rented accommodation

- Married couple living in your own home or a rented apartment

- Family member sharing with others

It applies to the space you currently occupy. Remember that feng shui relates to time, as well as space. When you go on holiday, your hotel room IS your home, on a temporary basis.

If you go camping, your tent IS your home, while you use it.

If you drive a mobile home or caravan around on holiday, that mobile home IS your present space.

The easiest way to think of it is, if you are paying for the space, it is yours for the time that you have paid for it.

This means that if you rent out a room in your house, it ceases to be yours for the time for which you have accepted the money.

DOES IT TAKE A LOT OF TIME?

Basics

Doing the 'Changes for the Year' is crucial if you want to get good results from feng shui quickly. It may take only 5 minutes to do. At worst, it might be a couple of hours.

It depends on whether you have a green plant to hand, and whether you have mirrors and red objects in the Shar Chi area for the year. You do not necessarily have to have a 6 hollow tubed metal wind chime. It may be, though, that this makes the ideal adjustment in your particular circumstances.

N.B. Doing the 'Changes for the Year' is essential if you are involved in any sort of law-suit and/or are going through a divorce.

As mentioned previously, feng shui is about both time and space. Doing the 'Changes for the Year' accounts for the most basic time element, the yearly journey of the Sun around the heavens. More advanced students also look at the monthly influences.

Just doing the 'Changes for the Year' and clutter clearing may be all that is necessary for you to start getting real life results.

Obviously, clutter clearing depends on what you already have in your home. On its most basic level it is about being able to move easily throughout your home or office. This means that the stairways, halls and corridors are clear. Also, all the objects on view are ones that you at least like (preferably love), and are useful.

Intermediate Level

This may take you a couple of months, doing things gradually over time. It is quite normal for people to take 2 months to complete all the changes recommended in a feng shui consultation. You may find that to follow all the suggestions in this book, you need to do little changes consistently over this kind of time frame.

Advanced Level

You sweep your space observationally on a daily basis and make little adjustments depending on what is happening in your life, and what is currently important. At this level of knowledge, you are also aware of what the 'Monthly Flying Stars' are, and make small corrections to allow for this.

Usually my advice is that, unless you are currently involved in events and decision making crucial to your long-term future, just getting the 'Changes for the Year' right is more than enough.

IS IT EXPENSIVE TO MAKE THE CHANGES?

Again, this depends on what you already have available in your home. 'Changes for the Year' require at least 1 green plant and/or a 6 hollow-tubed metal wind chime. This would mean a minimum cost of $30 – $40 (£15 – £25).

Doing bathroom corrections, would be approximately $16 (£10), per bathroom as you will need a small round convex mirror for the outside of each bathroom/toilet door and at least 1 red flowering, green plant per bathroom as a minimum.

If your home is not an even shape, i.e. a square or rectangle, you will need 2 mirrors and 2 pictures to go behind them OR 2 round glass faceted crystal balls OR 1 mirror and 1 picture and 1 round glass faceted crystal ball AND/OR fencing of some description, OR stones to mark out and enclose an area.

Depending on the cost of your mirrors and the size of round glass faceted crystal balls you use, a minimum cost would probably be in the region of $60. Stones to mark out an area may be cheaper then fencing. This will all depend on the amounts required.

So, for an even shaped property with 2 bathrooms, the absolute minimum cost is approximately $60 (£40).

For an uneven shape of property with 2 bathrooms, the absolute minimum cost would be approximately $100 (£70).

Remember that these are estimates made at the time of publication!

This assumes that you have at least 3 to 4 pictures/photographs/art works and/or sculptures and also at least 2 separate lamps or lights apart from standard main room ceiling lights.

If you have existing mirrors, plants and art work that you can use, you may not need to spend anything apart from your time re-arranging your existing items.

WHAT IF MY OTHER HALF DOESN'T BELIEVE IN IT?

One of the basic rules of feng shui is:

'Husband and wife must agree!'

(Please readers, do not fall about laughing!)

Basically, it doesn't matter whether you are married or not, or whether you are same sex partners – the rule still applies!

In an ideal world, this would mean that both of you like everything that is in your shared space. If each partner is lucky enough to have a room of their own, this is fairly easy to do. Anything your partner does not like just lives in your own room.

This becomes a little bit more challenging when there is less space. This is often the case for those of us who are city dwellers.

The message that you send to your partner when you keep this rule is extremely powerful. It says, in effect, 'You mean more to me than any material object'.

It follows on from this that if you are about to make a change that your partner really does not like, you negotiate and/or find an alternative.

There is only one area in which I would make an exception to this rule. Mirrors in a couple's bedroom cause interference by outside forces in your love life. This can be interference from in-laws, friends, relatives, a child, children or, worst case scenario, another lover.

It is usually possible to fit a large mirror inside one of your cupboard doors, provided this does not fall in the 'Changes for the Year' compass sector.

Usually, there are other mirrors, often in the bathroom, that can be used. It is really worth tactfully negotiating with your partner on this.

The main thing to remember with the 'Husband and Wife' must agree rule is that it means no sales talk! If you like something you like it. If you don't like it, you don't like it. It is as simple as preferring vanilla ice-cream to strawberry.

There is nothing inherently wrong with anything that you like or dislike, and the same goes for your partner. Nowhere is this more important than in the choice of a new home. This is ideally something that you both agree on from Day 1!

Real life often involves compromises. However, the minimum requirement here is that both parties at least **like** the property. 'Tolerate' or 'put up with' is not good enough. This is the sort of compromise that can lead to problems later on, and is best avoided.

The key issue is not whether your other half believes in feng shui or not. The issue is that they at least like the changes that you make to your shared space.

Getting Started

" A journey of a thousand miles begins with a single step. "

Lao-tzu
Chinese philosopher 604 BC – 531 BC

Chapter 2
Getting Started

FOR THE RELATIVELY CONTENT AND JUST CURIOUS READER...

At the beginning of any journey, you need to know where you are and where you would like to go.

Perhaps you just have a general interest in feng shui, and are curious to see whether it makes a difference in your life, as far as your general luck is concerned.

If this is the case, proceed slowly and cautiously. If your life is already more or else the way you like it, i.e. you are in a good relationship, your health is good, you like your work 70% of the time, and you are making enough money to live on, you are already in a relatively fortunate position.

You are working from a good base line. You know this because your life is witness to it.

There is an adage:

'If it isn't broke, DON'T FIX IT!'

This is very relevant to your particular situation. It is best to start with clutter clearing and small general improvements in each room. Make the assumption that your space is mostly OK from a feng shui perspective. In your case, less is definitely more. It is a case of tweaking, rather than making major alterations.

Your 'to do' list, would ideally be as follows:

- Do the 'Changes for the Year'.

- Clear your clutter and all passageways through your home/office.

- Do bathroom corrections.

- Balance the space if you are in an irregular shaped apartment or building.

- Correct for drain covers.

- Light the corners of each room and make small aesthetically pleasing upgrades to your space.

This means that you may want to read the chapters in the following order:

Chapter Four	Changes for the Year
Chapter Three	Clearing the clutter
Chapter Seven	How to balance your space…
Chapter Ten	A bit more detail! – bathroom corrections
Chapter Six	Recessed man-hole covers

You are likely to get much better results by following this sequence. You actually do have something to lose, i.e. your present positive state of balance. This makes it more important for you, than for someone who is facing a number of challenges, to follow a simple, logical sequence.

For most people, just doing the Changes for the Year and clearing their clutter is enough to produce noticeable improvements in good luck, especially financial luck!

FOR THE READER WITH PARTICULAR LIFE CHALLENGES...

Every home or office can be divided into the 9 areas of the Bagua. Please see the illustrations below.

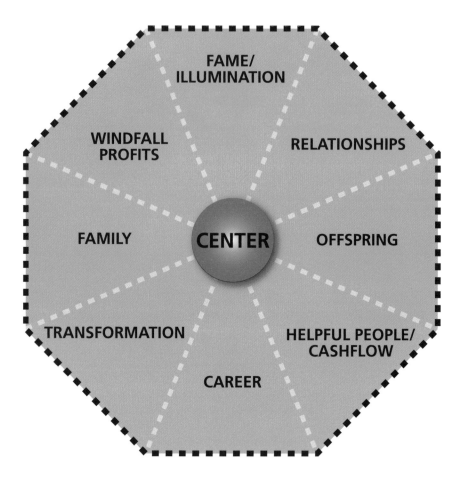

If you have particular life challenges, for the best results, you need to identify what areas of the Bagua relate to them specifically.

To give you some examples:

Perhaps you have satisfying work, but never seem to be able to sustain a good relationship. The **'Relationship/Marriage'** area of the Bagua is important for you.

Perhaps you have a wonderful love life and/or a wonderful family life, but find that you are going deeper into debt every month. You have a wonderful home that is appreciating in value. This means that with regard to assets and wealth, you have **'Windfall Profits/Fortunate Blessings'**. Your area of challenge is **'Cash Flow'** or the **'Heaven'** space.

Do you work in any branch of show business? Are you an artist or creative person? Is a degree of fame important for you to make a living at all? In your particular case, the **'Fame/Illumination'** area of the Bagua is vital.

Usually, the **'Cash Flow'** or **'Heaven'** space is also very relevant to you, as this area relates to your agent! If you haven't got one, start the process to get one immediately! Creative people are seldom blessed with the skills to market themselves to the necessary degree.

Feng shui is about easy changes and 'going with the flow'. Fortunately, great agents with wonderful deal-making skills already exist here on earth. Activating the **'Heaven'** areas in your home makes it easier for you to find the right one for you.

Do you find it hard to save money, and are you without any major assets, i.e. a home of your own, a savings plan and a retirement plan? If this is you, your area of challenge is **'Fortunate Blessings'**. This relates to large amounts of money – certainly enough to buy a house/apartment.

Is your major concern your physical well-being? Do you have health issues? If so, the **'Tai Chi/Health'** area in the center of your home is important for you.

Do you have problems with your relatives? Do you have a dispute going on with your neighbors? Have you just moved, and find yourself trying to get accepted into a new community? Are you trying to climb the corporate ladder? If any, or all of these apply to you, the **'Family'** area of the Bagua in your home is the one that needs your attention.

Are you not really sure where you want to be in the next year, 2 years, 3 years or 5 years? Do you have the feeling that you are drifting in life, or marking time? If this is the case, then the area of your home to check falls in the **'Career'** area of the Bagua.

Are you having trouble conceiving? Are your children problematic? Do you have writers block? Are you finding it difficult to express yourself creatively? In your case the **'Offspring/Creativity'** area of the Bagua is where you need to focus your feng shui.

Are you studying? Is it important for you to pass examinations to secure your future? Are you having trouble passing your driving test? In all of these cases, the **'Transformation/Knowledge'** area of the Bagua is important for you.

Are you dealing with 3 or more areas of challenge in your life?
Is this one of the reasons that you picked this book to read?
Are you at a turning point or crisis point in your life?
Are you going through a divorce?
Are you about to be fired or made redundant?

If the answer to any of these questions is 'yes', after you have done the general base line things, i.e. Changes for the Year, clearing clutter, and bathroom and drain cover corrections, you need to concentrate on getting the **'Transformation/Knowledge'** area of your home in good order.

Some other questions that will lead you to the right areas of the Bagua to enhance are the following:

What would ideally be happening in your life over the next year?

If you can't answer this question or have difficulty with it, then you need to focus on the **'Career'** area of the Bagua.

What absolutely must happen in your life in the next year?

Again, if you are not sure or are having a problem defining this, then you need to focus on the 'Career' area of the Bagua.

What is most important to you:

Health	–	relates to the Tai Chi/Center of the Bagua
Wealth	–	relates to Windfall Profits/Fortunate Blessings for large amounts of money and/or the Helpful People/Heaven area for cash flow
Harmony	–	relates to the Relationships/Marriage area of the Bagua
or all 3?	–	relates to the Transformation/Knowledge area of the Bagua

What areas of your home do you like the most?

This will usually relate to areas of the Bagua and compass directions concerning things that are going well in your life. There may be things that you are taking for granted.

What area(s) do you like the least?

These are likely to relate to your most demanding areas of life. You are most likely to have your best results when you have made enough changes to these area(s) to make them attractive to you.

Is your home an even shape? i.e. a square or rectangle?

If the answer is 'no' you are likely to find that the missing space is in an area where you are challenged.

A missing space in either **'Windfall Profits/Fortunate Blessings'** and/or the **'Heaven'** space is likely to result in financial problems.

A missing space in either **'Relationship/Marriage'** or **'Transformation/ Knowledge'** is likely to make it difficult for a man to attract a good relationship with a woman. Both these areas are female spaces.

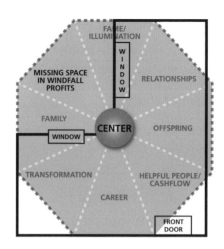

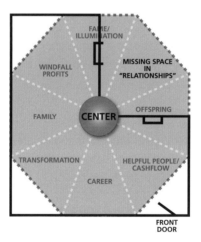

'Transformation/Knowledge' also relates to your relationship with yourself. When you love yourself, it is easy to relate to other people. This is a pre-requisite for good intimate relationships.

Who do you live with and how do they affect your life?

If you are in a family situation, you need to sort out your own personal space first, i.e. your own room.

If you share your apartment with others, again, your own room and/or your own possessions are your first priorities.

If you share an apartment, your room is 70% of your feng shui. Harmony with your fellow sharers is more important than short comings in their house-keeping and washing up skills!

If you do not even have a room of your own, sort out whatever space you do have, and make it clean, clear and uncluttered. Remember that harmony with those you live with is an over-arching principle of feng shui.

How much clutter do you have in your home/office?

Feng shui is not a conspiracy to get you to do more housework, and tidy up for no reason! The whole purpose of creating order is so that it is quick and easy to find things, and move through your life with minimum stress.

You have probably already noticed that really wealthy people usually have a well-ordered environment, both at home and at work.

In the areas of your life that you most enjoy, it is highly likely that you already have a great deal of order. Creating that same order in your areas of challenge is one of the easiest, and also least expensive ways of attracting positive circumstances into your life.

Clearing the Clutter

" Order is the 1st law of the Universe. "

Anon

Chapter 3
Clearing the Clutter!

WHAT EXACTLY IS CLUTTER?

The dictionary definition of clutter is "a crowded, untidy collection of things".

This is interesting in itself! This assumes that you have even bothered to collect things together in one place…

I would like to offer you another definition of clutter as being 'anything that you no longer use or love'. It may be, that not only do you not use it, but you never liked it in the first place!

Generally speaking, you will find that in areas of your life that work well, you will naturally have order. If your family is a priority, you probably have all their birthdays neatly listed somewhere, on your phone, your computer or in your diary.

If you have a hobby, most probably all the books you have relating to this hobby will be somewhere where you can find them, pretty much instantly.

If you feel overwhelmed by the amount of clutter cleaning you want to do, start by noticing where you already have order.

Just in case you have a problem even considering a tidy-up…

HOW TO DECIDE WHAT TO KEEP, WHAT TO RECYCLE AND WHAT TO THROW AWAY

Clearing clutter means that you will have to choose one of the above categories for each item.

Of course, if it is an item that you love and use, the decision is very simple. It stays, and then you only need to find a place for it.

WHAT ABOUT ITEMS THAT YOU ARE UNCLEAR ABOUT?

This is why people often have so much resistance to actually get down to clutter clearing. Very often, they have problems making decisions anyway OR they need to go through a lengthy process to make any decision at all OR the items in question carry a strong emotional charge for them.

In all of these scenarios, the key question to ask yourself is, 'What exactly am I saving this for?' Other useful questions are: 'Have I used or worn this item in the last 12 months?' and 'Am I likely to use or wear this in the next 12 months?'

When you feel a lot of emotion about releasing an item, you can be sure that examining your feelings and coming to a decision produces powerful results.

The usual suggestion is to have 3 boxes labelled 'keep', 'chuck' and 'maybe'.

It is usually easy to decide on the items you want to keep, unless you have so much stuff that some things will need to go into storage.

Anything that you hate, and this includes gifts from people who may no longer be your friends, definitely goes into 'chuck'. Also to be included are gifts that you don't like that have come from relatives.

EVERYTHING ELSE IS 'MAYBE'

In terms of clothing, anything that you have not worn for a year, really needs to go in the 'chuck' pile. That is unless you know you will be wearing it within the next 3 months.

Many women have 'fat' clothes and 'thin' clothes, and then clothes that they wear all the time. The idea here is to go with the clothes you wear all the time and recycle the others. After all, when you lose 85 pounds you deserve some new clothes!

The other thing to remember is that it is perfectly OK for you to sell your unwanted items. In fact, this may be an excellent temporary source of income for you! If you can't be bothered selling them, giving them away is also fine. Even clothes in really poor condition can be recycled as rags.

What is also very interesting is finding out about the things that you do not want to give away, and yet you do not use. These items will nearly always be connected to you at an identity level that is still important for you. For example, you may no longer work as a paramedic and yet find it difficult to recycle the uniform.

Another example of this might be a keen amateur golfer – a man who, through injury or ill health, has found that he can no longer play. Hanging on to his golf clubs may mean he is in denial about his health.

Another possible reason is that letting go of the golf clubs would signify to him that the illness or injury has won, and he has lost.

His best way around this is to actually let the golf clubs go, with the thought that when it is possible to play again, he will easily afford a new set of clubs. Meanwhile, he does not have the golf clubs lying around reminding him of what he cannot do, while he engages in other less physically demanding hobbies.

So far, so good! You have the 'keep' box for what is definitely staying and the 'chuck' box for what is definitely going. What happens to the 'maybes'?

I would suggest that you do not even approach the 'maybes' until you have found a home for all the items in the 'keep' box, and have given away, recycled or sold all the items in the 'chuck' box.

All the items in the 'maybe' box now get re-classified in exactly the same way. The amusing thing about this is, that having gone through the process once, it does become easier the second time around.

It is completely normal to go through this process 3, 4 or 5 times before all your clutter is cleared.

WHAT IF I AM A NATURALLY MESSY PERSON?

Even the messiest person has order somewhere.

What do you love?

What is already organized in your life?

You may already have your own version of order within chaos.

How does your disorder impact on other people in your life?

Can you find your passport within 5 minutes?

Are all your tax papers together?

Are all your bank statements together?

Where in your life at present would more organization most help you?

HOW TO CLEAR THE CLUTTER WITH MINIMAL EFFORT

It helps greatly if you limit yourself to only 7½ minutes a day to clutter clearing. Play some inspiring, joyful music to accompany this.

One of my very untidy colleagues gave this advice to one of her, also very untidy, clients, with dramatic results. In 7½ minutes a day, within the space of 3 weeks, this client radically altered her own environment for the better. The results in her life were also quite amazing. She created some fabulous work opportunities for herself that she had previously considered out of her reach.

SPACE CLEARING TO CLEAN AND CLEAR THE ATMOSPHERE

Space clearing usually refers to lifting the invisible atmospheres that linger in a room or a house over time, because of the events that have taken place there. People's strong emotions frequently leave a resonance behind.

Although space clearing is also about spirit release, it would, in my opinion, be very foolish to attempt this without experience, and on your own. If you suspect that there is a spirit presence attached to your home or office, ask for help from an experienced psychic, shaman or priest.

This is about more than improving the atmosphere of your home. It is about helping a soul move forward to a better place in the space /time continuum.

Just as there are attendants here on the physical plane when we are born to help us arrive, so there are guides whose job it is to assist the souls of the departed.

Laws apply in the spirit world as they do on Earth. Spirit guides are only permitted to help us here when we specifically request it.

"Ask, and you shall receive" – In this instance, if in doubt, get as much help as possible, from both the physical and spiritual planes!

Let's assume that your intention is just to improve the atmosphere of your home.

There are a number of different ways of space clearing. The following are the most popular:

1. Have a party. The loud music, dancing and celebrations usually break up any old energy patterns that may be lingering.

2. Use sound, especially reverberating deep base tones from a guitar or electric organ.
   Use a bell or bells. Stand in each corner, and ring the bell from floor to ceiling.
   Stand in the center of the room and ring the bell so that it resonates, and you can hear the harmonic tones.

3. Smudge the room with slow-burning sage.
   Use a feather or a fan to waft the smoke into each corner of the room, from floor to ceiling.
   Stand in the middle of the room and waft the smoke out to the corners and the walls of the room.
   Go along each wall and waft the smoke up it from floor to ceiling.

4. Visualize white light slowly filling the room, and then visualize a soft pink light filling the room, and visualize the white light filling the room again.

5. Burn incense and candles in the room.

6. Sing songs and/or chant mantras in the room.

7. Spray special, space clearing flower remedies round the room.

8. Fill the room with flowers and plants as this has a positive effect on both the psychic atmosphere and the air quality.

9. Leave small amounts of ordinary salt in the corners and the center of the room.

10. Place clear quartz crystals, programmed with your intent to clear the space, in the room. Wash them in cold running water after a day or two and leave them out in sunlight afterwards for at least 3 hours.

11. If you have a good connection with the spirit world yourself, ask the spirits and guides that work with you to clear the room, and set positive energies there on your behalf.
Remember to say both 'please' and 'thank you!' It is very important to acknowledge any help that you receive.
Remember if you would like help from spirit guides, you need to clearly request it before they can act for you.

12. Pray and meditate, if you have a spiritual practice, as this alters the energy in any room for the better.

THE REWARDS! SOME OF THE INTERESTING RESULTS THAT HAVE HAPPENED AFTER CLUTTER CLEARING

People find money
Some sell items which fund holidays and pay off credit cards
Some get given new clothes, books and DVDs
Some sell their home
Some find their new home

Space clearing generated enough money for one client to pay for major building work and renovations. This was because, in the process, the history relating to an item that his family decided to sell was discovered. This information or 'provenance', as the antique dealers call it, significantly increased its value.

The advantages of clearing clutter and creating order are:

■ You create space for something new to manifest.

■ You create time to do more fun things (rather then search for clean underwear).

- Frequently you find money down the back of chairs and in clothes.

- If you are planning to move, it seems to speed up the process of finding somewhere new.

Changes for
the Year

" Your point of power is always in the present. "

Seth channelled by Jane Roberts, author of
"Seth Speaks"
May 8, 1929 – Sept 5, 1984

Chapter 4
Changes for the Year

THE MOST IMPORTANT FENG SHUI ADJUSTMENT YOU CAN MAKE FOR GOOD RESULTS!

When you get used to living in balanced space, you will notice interesting things happen at the end of one Chinese year, going into the next Chinese New Year. You may find that suddenly little things are not going quite right, and there are a lot of minor irritations.

Some examples of this would be:

1. Getting a parking ticket when you are usually meticulous about where you park your car

2. Having a number of cancellations in your appointment schedule if you are self-employed

3. Finding that you are dealing with a greater than average number of breakages and repairs in your home and

4. Equipment malfunctioning

This is even more likely to be true if you have done the changes for the departing year. As the energies shift for the incoming Chinese New Year, the temporary imbalance that this causes becomes more noticeable.

To get the best results from feng shui, you need to take both time and space into account. If you omit the time element, you may find yourself 'out of sync' with what is happening around you. This is likely to result in a lot of outside interference with your plans.

The Chinese view is that every year, negative energies come from 1 of the 8 compass directions or from the center itself. From the 3rd February 2012, it is the Year of the Dragon, and the direction of negative energy or 'Shar Chi' energy (as it is also called) is considered to come from the South East.

WHY WOULD YOU WANT TO DO 'CHANGES FOR THE YEAR?'

To get the best results from the feng shui adjustments you make, as well as emphasizing the positive, it is also necessary to minimize the negative.

You do 'Changes for the Year' with the intention of stopping external influences, i.e. people and organizations, getting in your way.

This enables you to go forward in your life with minimum resistance, and allows for the fact that, any time you attempt to create something new, just dealing with your own inner resistance, never mind anybody else's, is more than enough.

HOW TO DO 'CHANGES FOR THE YEAR'

The Shar Chi, or negative energy, is considered to be a form of **Earth** energy.

Therefore, using the 'Creative Cycle' of the 5 elements (shown below) we can use the element of **Metal** to 'drain' the negative **Earth** energy.

It works like this.

There are basic 5 elements:

Earth, Metal, Water, Wood, Fire

In the 'Creative Cycle', each element feeds or nourishes the next element in the cycle. It follows on from this that each element 'drains' the preceding element.

Therefore:

Metal drains **Earth**, **Water** drains **Metal**, **Wood** drains **Water**, **Fire** drains **Wood**, **Earth** drains **Fire**

Following on from this it is easy to understand that a 6 hollow tubed metal wind chime can be used to 'drain' the negative **Earth** (Shar Chi) area.

There is also a 'Destructive Cycle', where each element controls or 'kills' the

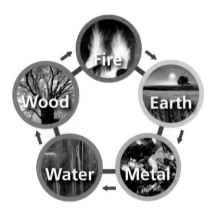

2nd one going clockwise round the circle. This element itself is controlled or 'killed' by the 2nd element away from it going anti-clockwise round the circle. Please refer to the diagram below.

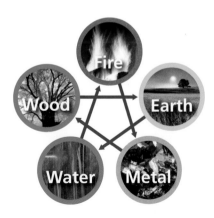

Earth controls **Water**
Water controls **Fire**
Fire controls **Metal**
Metal controls **Wood**
Wood controls **Earth**

As **Wood** controls or 'kills' **Earth**, and Shar Chi energy is a form of **Earth** energy, we can use a green plant in the Shar Chi area instead of a wind chime to do the 'Changes for the Year'.

Bearing this in mind, 'Changes for the Year' involve removing:

1. all red objects and any objects that are bright orange, or could be considered flame colored (because fire feeds earth)

2. round glass faceted crystal balls (because they are energy magnifiers)

3. cut glass crystal (for the same reason)

4. mirrors (even more so, for the same reason) from the Shar Chi area and

5. placing a 6 hollow tubed metal wind chime OR a large green plant in the Shar Chi area

Remember, you are making these changes to disperse the negative energy of the Shar Chi area. You need to do this even if the direction of the Shar Chi area happens to be one of your best ones.

This rule of feng shui takes precedence over everything else. It is time sensitive and lasts for 1 year only.

Also, be aware that it is most inadvisable to have a wind chime and a mirror in the same room, even if the mirror falls in a different compass sector.

Both wind chimes and mirrors are very powerful cures. However, while the mirror accentuates energy, the wind chime dissipates it. Having both of these powerful cures in one room is likely to produce chaotic, rather than pleasant results.

You both attract and repel at the same time. In real life, a very common example of this is someone getting plenty of job interviews, but never actually being offered the job.

If there is a TV in the Shar Chi area, use a plant rather than a wind chime, as TV screens can function as mirrors. NEVER hang the wind chime in the center of a room. It needs to be sited at a window, pick one that is pleasant sounding to you.

If you have concerns about money and, specifically, cash flow, using a 6 hollow tubed metal wind chime, rather than one with 5 chimes, produces a better effect. The reason for this is that 6 relates to the **'Heaven/Helpful People'** area, which is also concerned with cash flow. Please see Chapter 6.

Also, NEVER cover a mirror in the Shar Chi area, and think that you have done the 'Changes for the Year'. The result of doing this is that negative events come towards you, and you are unaware of them, often until it is too late to take evasive or preventative action.

If you really cannot remove the mirror, a make-shift cure is to ensure that you reflect a lot of green objects, preferably green plants, in the mirror. If you are dealing with a divorce or a law suit of any description, it is always better to actually remove the mirror.

The more money that is at stake and/or the more crucial the situation is, the more this applies.

WHERE AND WHEN TO DO THE 'CHANGES FOR THE YEAR' FOR THE NEXT 9 YEARS

Chinese New Year usually occurs around the end of January and beginning of February each year.

It is a good idea to take the changes for the previous year down by the 2nd week of January, at the latest, so that you are ready for the changes for the new Chinese year.

The following list shows which compass sectors house the Shar Chi area over the next 9 years:

2012	–	South East
2013	–	The Center of your home
2014	–	North West
2015	–	West
2016	–	North East
2017	–	South
2018	–	North
2019	–	South West
2020	–	East

A living green plant (and preferably a large one!) is a good substitute, if you don't like wind chimes. This may also be a more appropriate solution if the sound of the chimes bothers your neighbors. Harmony is paramount!

You may be wondering if you can still use a wind chime when it needs to go in a compass sector where metal is unfavorable in relationship to your own Kua number. Please see Chapter 10 – 'Numerology'.

The answer to this is, that as 'Changes for the Year' take precedence over everything else, it is up to you to choose what you prefer. A metal wind chime or a large, green plant are both equally fine.

HOW TO TAKE A COMPASS READING

As the 'Changes for the Year' are so important, it follows that getting your compass reading right is essential.

Make sure that you are standing in the center of your home, more about that later. Because you are looking at 8 compass sectors and the central space, accuracy is vital. It is not enough to say "The Sun goes down over there, so this must be West." It is surprising how small each sector is when you measure inside a building.

A very simple compass is fine, although an orienteering one is more precise. To start with, you can use the compass on your mobile phone, if it has that facility. Choose magnetic rather than true North for this reading and always double check your results with an ordinary compass later.

For an accurate reading, you need to minimise any magnetic interference. This involves removing metal in the form of jewelry and watches from your person . Make sure that your mobile phone is not on you either, unless you are using it to take the reading. This is because mobile phones emit electro-magnetic frequencies.

Place the compass in the palm of your hand. A compass is fundamentally a base or body with a floating needle in the center of it. Wait for the floating needle to stop moving. Where the red arrow of the needle points is North.

Gently rotate the body of the compass so that the N for North lines up with where the arrow is pointing. This gives you your reading for North. You can now read off from the compass all the other sectors.

HOW TO FIND THE GEOMETRIC CENTER OF YOUR HOME

This is easy if you live in a square or rectangular shaped building. Simply draw straight diagonal lines from each top corner to each bottom corner. Please see the diagram below.

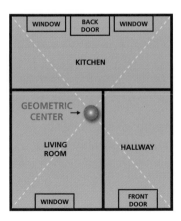

WHAT IF YOU HAVE OUTBUILDINGS, PERHAPS A GARAGE?

If you are in an odd shaped building and/or you have a garage and/or several out buildings, then you need to do the following, so that you find the geometric center of your home precisely:

Any smaller buildings, i.e. a garage or a large shed within 120 foot (35 meters, approximately) of your home, need to be included in the calculation.

1. You find the geometric center for each building by drawing diagonal lines from the corners, as shown in the diagrams below.

2. Join up these 2 centers and find the mid-point on this line. This gives you the geometric center of the buildings together.

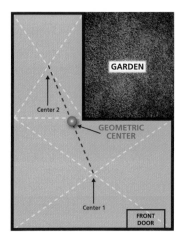

If you have more than 1 outbuilding, the method is similar. Do the following:

3. Find the geometric center of each building and join these centers up. Then find the mid-point between these 2 and join it to the 3rd center and find the mid-point of that line. (Please see examples below).

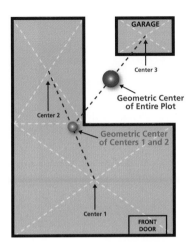

WHAT IF YOUR HOME IS AN ODD SHAPE?

Perhaps it appears to have a piece missing. In this case:

4. Divide your space into 2 or more rectangles.

5. Find the geometric center of each.

6. Join the geometric centers together with 1 line.

7. The mid-point of this line is the geometric center of your home.

If your home divides into more than 2 rectangles or squares, follow the same procedure as above and then join the mid-points together sequentially so that you arrive at a final mid-point, which is the geometric center. Please see the example on the next page.

Remember that you are doing this to pinpoint the Shar Chi area accurately. It is worth it to stop outside negative interference in your life.

Some authorities consider that you do not need to take out buildings more than 120ft or 40 meters away from your home into consideration. However, if you do you may well find that the geometric center falls outside your house and/or the boundaries of your land.

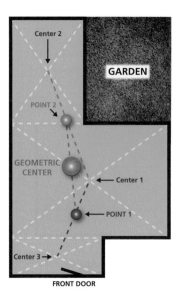

My own experience in these cases shows that there is an effect.

I have seen situations where there is a garage belonging to the property 1 or 2 houses away. This usually translates into the person not having as much control over their own life and circumstances as they would like.

The way around this is fairly simple, as long as you do not need the garage. Rent it out or sell it. Once you have taken money for the use of a space, it is, in feng shui terms, no longer yours.

STORIES TAKEN FROM REAL LIFE

Some real life examples of people who did not do 'Changes for the Year' or did not do them correctly:

A very hard working executive was under continuing pressure from a new director who had arrived from another division of the company abroad. The new director had not fully familiarized himself with conditions in this country, and continued to pressurize my client, the executive.

This appeared to be a classic example of outside obstruction in my client's life. He was doing his job, in fact, above and beyond the call of duty, while also having to run interference from a higher up who had insufficient local knowledge.

The solution in this case was to do the 'Changes for the Year' thoroughly and correctly, and, fortunately, the situation resolved itself.

The result of covering a mirror in the Shar Chi area for the year:

One client found out that her boyfriend had been seeing another lover for over 3 months before she was even aware of the situation. It could be argued that perhaps this was a good thing, in that she did eventually find out that he was not the man for her. Her preference would have been to have had some advance warning.

While doing feng shui in your home cannot control anyone else's behavior, done correctly, it can at least attract the necessary information to you.

Benefits from doing 'Changes for the Year'...

Your plans proceed smoothly and you move towards your goals quicker.

All the other feng shui cures you do are much more effective.

And finally...

ALWAYS remember to move the wind chime out of the Shar Chi area of the preceding year, before you put one up in the Shar Chi area for the new Chinese New Year.

Remember, wind chimes disperse energy. If you have not taken the wind chime down for the preceding year, you may find that you are dispersing money, friends or job opportunities, when you would really rather not!

Health

" The first wealth is health. "

Ralph Waldo Emerson
May 25, 1803 – April 27, 1882

Chapter 5
Health

Conventional feng shui regards 3 things as being relevant to your health:

1. THE CENTER

This central area of your space should, ideally, be clean, clear and uncluttered, and well lit.

What is in the center of your home?

First of all, find the exact center of your home using the information from Chapter 4.

Is there a flow of energy in this space?

Ideally, the space in the center of your home is empty, allowing for movement through it. An overhead light in this position is of positive benefit.

If the center of your home falls in your bathroom, the feng shui 'cure' for this is to mirror all 4 walls. In this case it is not 'war of the mirrors'. All the adults in the house should be able to see their head and shoulders in these mirrors. Position the mirrors high enough up so that they do NOT reflect the toilet.

In every household I have visited where this has been the case, there have been serious money problems.

In one case, where there were 2 bathrooms in the household, the money situation dramatically improved when the toilet that was reflected in the mirror was removed for repair!

In other areas of the Bagua, and where there is more than one bathroom in the house, some feng shui experts recommend not using this room at all.

However, the **Center** is of special importance and takes precedence over everything else. Shutting up a bathroom in the central space creates stagnation and difficulties, far in excess of those you are trying to correct.

This is especially true if you are trying to move home. You need to create a flow of fresh air and people through this area.

Is the Center well lit, clean and clear?

Just leaving the light on in this area for a minimum of 3 hours a day or night symbolically adds the element of **Fire**, and is an inexpensive feng shui cure itself.

Historically, in the West, we have usually had a light in the center of the ceiling of each room.

2.   THE POSITION OF YOUR BED IN THE BEDROOM

In practice, the most important consideration, to do with the position of your bed with regards to your health, is about the energies around it and under it – **Earth** energies and electromagnetic energies. We will deal with this later on in this chapter.

Classical feng shui has 4 main concerns about the position of your bed:

- which direction your head points in when you sleep

- that you have support behind you when you sleep, i.e. a wall and not a window, and that you have a headboard for your bed

- that you have a good line of sight from your bed to the door so that you can clearly see anyone coming in to your bedroom

- that there are no overhead beams or rafters above you when you sleep (correct for this by draping soft fabric around and over the beams)

The best position is diagonally opposite the door, so that you can clearly see anyone coming into the room. Remember, our ancestors frequently lived in a state of war!

Bear in mind though, that, regarding your health, if this puts you over geopathic stress, you are better off moving your bed to what is considered to be a less desirable position.

Your health is always number 1 on the list.

3. YOUR COMPASS DIRECTION FOR LONGEVITY

In Chinese, this is called 'Tien Yi'. This translates as 'Heavenly Doctor' and is sometimes referred to as 'lengthening years'.

In order to find this, you will need to calculate your Kua number. Please see Chapter 10.

If health is your top priority, ideally have your head pointing towards your 'Heavenly Doctor' compass direction.

If this is not possible, any of your good directions will be helpful, provided that there is no counter-indication for the present year (please see page 167).

You can enhance this compass sector by adding the element of **Fire**.

Do this by:

- keeping an electric light on

- burning candles and/or incense

- using red and/or flame colored objects in the decor

Then we have…

21st Century energy considerations regarding health

1.   GOOD FOOD AND FRESH WATER

The importance of clean air, clean water (feng shui = wind water) and fresh food is a given.

Conventionally cooked, rather than microwaved food, is preferable as microwaving changes the rotation of half of the water molecules in the food from left to right.

All living beings on our planet are composed exclusively of left rotated molecules, and, bear in mind, we are 70% water.

2.   ELECTROMAGNETIC ENERGIES AND GETTING A GOOD NIGHT'S SLEEP

Modern feng shui takes into account the often unrecognized, and frequently crucial influence of the different types of **Earth** energies and electromagnetic fields on human beings. These can be supportive, neutral or draining.

While the energies around you during the day have an effect on your well-being, those you experience while you are sleep are even more significant. This is because during this time your body re-charges like a battery from the Earth's electromagnetic field.

For this reason, the position of your bed and the energies around it are most important.

To get a good night's sleep, you may need to do more than just following conventional wisdom.

Avoiding a lot of tea or coffee in the evening (research has shown that even 1 cup of coffee in the morning can cause insomnia in some people!) and taking time to wind down mentally are useful habits.

If this does not work for you, you may need to remove all electrical appliances from your bedroom, including the TV. At the very least, position them 6 feet (approximately 2 meters) away from your bed.

Why?

Our bodies are made up of approximately 70% water, which is an excellent conductor of electricity. We are also electromagnetic creatures. The acupuncture meridians in our bodies describe paths of bio-electromagnetic energy. Nearby electrical equipment, and sleeping over geopathic stress or vortex energy, can disrupt this bio-electromagnetic flow to varying extents.

Electrical equipment here includes wi-fi and broadband equipment, radio alarm clocks, stereos, TVs and cell (mobile) phones on charge. TVs continue to emit electrical frequencies even when they are on standby. This is why it is better to forego having a television in your bedroom altogether, if health is a major issue for you.

If you are having serious sleep problems, experiment with removing all electrical equipment from your bedroom, with the exception of lamps and lights, for 3 weeks.

After this time, you will know whether electromagnetic interference is causing your sleep problems or not.

If after doing all this, you are still not getting a good night's sleep, you may want to employ the services of a dowser to find out what the **Earth** energies are around your bed.

This will enable you to either move off any negative lines, or take the appropriate counter-measures described below.

3. EARTH ENERGIES AND THEIR EFFECTS ON YOUR HEALTH

Schumann Waves and why these are good for you

Schumann Waves were discovered by Professor W.O. Schumann in 1952. These are beneficial electromagnetic energy waves that vibrate between the Earth itself and various layers of the atmosphere.

Their frequency is very close to that of the alpha brain wave frequencies found in human beings when they are most relaxed. It is thought that they have positive effects on sleep patterns and hormonal cycles.

The first astronauts NASA sent up into space returned to Earth feeling tired and disorientated. They discovered that by incorporating Schumann Waves in the spacecraft, this problem was overcome.

It is also thought that the effects of jet lag may be due to a lack of Schumann Waves existing at the altitudes that passenger airlines fly. The metal fuselage of the aircraft further weakens the Schumann Waves there.

What is geopathic stress?

Geopathic stress can be defined as our reaction, as human beings, to any distortion of the Earth's electromagnetic energy field, outside the frequency of Schumann Waves (7.83 Hz).

Common physical factors associated with geopathic stress are:

- water pipes

- electricity

- tunnels

- underground railways

- underground streams

- mineral ores and

- geological faults

Some authorities also consider that subtle energies can cause geopathic stress as well.

Whatever its cause, if you are suffering from chronic health problems, recognizing the presence of geopathic stress is vitally important.

How does it affect you at home and work?

Without question, the impact geopathic stress has on you is directly related to how much time you spend in contact with it. Consequently, geopathic stress positioned under your bed will have a greater negative effect on your health than geopathic stress in a bathroom or garage, where you spend very little time.

Your cat, if you have one, may be showing you where it is

While geopathic stress has a negative effect on human beings, there are some creatures for whom it is absolutely wonderful. Cats will always position themselves over geopathic stress, if they can, as their energy fields positively charge from it.

There is every reason to get a dowser to check the energies around your bed, if your cat is constantly sleeping there, and you have health problems.

Hornets, wasps and ants also like geopathic stress. If you are having problems with infestations of any of these creatures, you may want to purchase a device to counter geopathic stress and/or increase Schumann Waves.

How to best deal with geopathic stress in your home and work place

The best way of dealing with geopathic stress, which is, after all, a natural occurring phenomenon, is to move off the line. This is, by far, the best solution.

Although you can buy devices that will deal with geopathic stress in different ways, all the manufacturers are clear that these machines do not provide a complete solution. It is, therefore, essential to dowse after plugging in any device to find out exactly where the energies have been altered, and where they have not!

When you use one of these devices, you are creating an area where there is a double frequency – the existing one and another frequency to counter-balance it.

This is less than desirable if you have health issues, unless you have absolutely no alternative.

Another way of dealing with this, is to communicate with the **Earth** elementals in your home or office. Ask them to move the geopathic stress, so that it does not pass through your bed or the area in which you sit. Be sure to thank them when this work is done, and to periodically check that the adjustment is still in place.

You may need to give the **Earth** elementals some sort of 'offering'. You may get the impression that they would like some semi-precious stones or crystals in a particular area to assist them. Do this as soon as possible while saying 'Thank You'.

Please bear in mind that all **Earth** energies are changeable phenomena. Road works and building works can alter **Earth** energies on a specific line for 5, 10 or even 25 miles away. This is why it is a good idea to check for geopathic stress periodically.

What is vortex energy?

Vortex energy spins horizontally. You can discover its presence by dowsing. Please see diagram below.

While this does not have the same negative health effects as geopathic stress, it is a de-stabilizing energy. Certainly, children tend to be hyperactive in its presence and adults tend to feel off-key.

The reason for this is that our bio-electromagnetic energy mainly circulates in a vertical plane, up our backs and down our fronts.

As you can imagine, putting a primarily vertical energy field, such as your own, into a horizontally spinning field, is bound to be somewhat disruptive.

How to correct for it

a)   If there are only adults in the house

There are 2 basic ways of correctly for vortex energy. For those who like a more physical method, place a clear upright quartz crystal over the vortex area. When you dowse, you will find that the field has been neutralized.

There is an upside and a downside to this method.

The upside is this works immediately, and provided you leave the crystal in place, it is a very stable cure.

If you have pets or children, and the crystal is knocked on its side, it ceases to be effective.

Also, it is inadvisable to have clear quartz crystals around children under the age of 13 as, if you do, you will find that the children tend to become more emotional and have a tendency to take over the household. Not good for them or for you!

b)   If you have children in the house

Provided no-one is sleeping, or spending a great deal of time over vortex energy, it is not a problem. However, if it is in an area where anyone sleeps, or, because of lack of space, is compelled to spend time, the best solution is to work with the **Earth** elementals and/or guardian spirit of the house.

Do the same as for geopathic stress. Ask for the vortex to be shifted to another dimension while you live or work there.

Remember to thank the invisible energy forces for their help, and also to check, from time to time, that the vortex is no longer there.

In common with most sentient beings, **Earth** elementals like to be noticed and appreciated for their work.

Wealth – A Few Definitions

" Wealth is not his that has it, but his that enjoys it. "

Benjamin Franklin
Jan 17, 1706 – Apr 17, 1790

Chapter 6
Wealth – A Few Definitions

Wealth –   "riches; being rich; abundance or a profusion of…"
            Quote: The Little Oxford Dictionary

Wealth –   "abundance, possessions or resources"
           "profusion"
            Quote: Webster American English Dictionary

Wealth –   "What you have left when you have lost all your money"
            Quote: Roger Hamilton, Wealth Dynamics, Entrepreneur

It is apparent, from looking at these definitions, that there is certainly more than one way to look at what wealth actually means.

Is it more valuable to have a fish or to know how to fish?

While there is no doubt that it is always useful to have the fish, obviously the long-term solution is to know how to fish.

This is one of the reasons why, when clients are challenged in a number of sectors of the Bagua, the most important area to enhance is the **'Transformation/Knowledge'** area.

For those only challenged by material abundance, the Bagua has 2 sectors that very specifically relate to wealth:

- the **'Windfall Profits'**, also known as **'Fortunate Blessings'** area and

- the **'Heaven'** area, also known as **'Helpful People'**

For those of us living in the West, the **'Windfall Profits'** or **'Fortunate Blessings'** area relates to large sums of money. Size matters here! Certainly the amount involved is enough to buy an extremely good car, put a deposit on a house, or buy the house outright. It also relates to large lottery wins.

For a farmer, this area could relate to a 'bumper' harvest, instead of, or including money.

The **'Heaven'** area, also known as the **'Helpful People'** area, relates specifically to cash flow. This is the money needed to pay the rent, mortgage and utility bills and keep food on the table.

It helps to decide which of these areas is more important to you, before making changes in your home.

If you have a good salary and no savings, you already have a positive cash flow situation in your life. It is the large money related to savings, pensions and home ownership that may be lacking. In your case, you would be looking at enhancing the **'Fortunate Blessings'** area.

If, on the other hand, you own your home outright but have a small monthly income, as is the case for many retired people, you already have a positive situation as regards **'Fortunate Blessings'** in your life. The area you would seek to enhance would be the **'Heaven'** or **'Helpful People'** area, which relates to cash flow.

Please refer to the diagram of the Bagua on page 28. As you can see, there are 9 sectors, each one relating to a particular life topic or situation.

HOW TO USE THE BAGUA

Use the Bagua as a template, and place it over a drawing of your home.

When you do this, ensure that your front door is in an area at the bottom of the page.

This means that when you place the Bagua over your drawing, the front door can only fall in one of 3 sectors:

Transformation/Knowledge
Career
Heaven/Helpful People

This form of feng shui using the Bagua is also known as the 3 Gate Method of Chi. The following diagrams show how to do this:

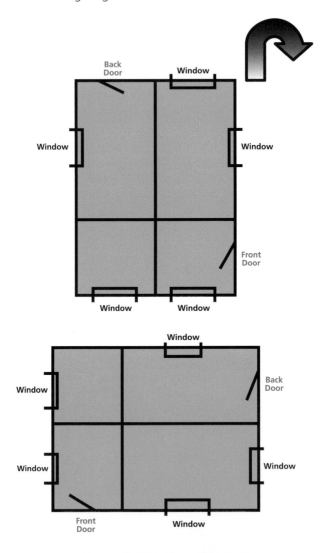

There are also some circumstances where you will need to track the front door down to the bottom of the page. Please see diagram for how this is done.

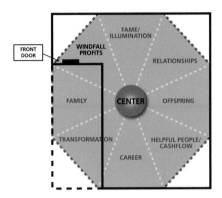

TRACKING THE FRONT DOOR DOWN TO THE BOTTOM OF THE PAGE

As you can see from the diagram, the front door actually falls in **'Windfall Profits/Fortunate Blessings'**. The purpose of tracking it back is to accurately place the Bagua over the floor plan. Remember, the bottom line must be the **'Transformation/Knowledge'**, **'Career'** and **'Cash Flow/ Helpful People'** areas of the Bagua.

WHICH DOOR IS THE FRONT DOOR?

Sometimes there is some confusion about which door is really the front door, especially if the back door is very frequently used by members of the family.

Ask yourself which door your postman uses to deliver the mail. This door is usually considered to be your front door, unless no-one else ever uses it.

In this case, take the door that everyone uses as your front door.

THE AREAS OF THE BAGUA:

'Career' relates to your path in life and general direction.

'**Relationships/Marriage**' is concerned with both friendships and sexual relationship/s.

'**Family/Elders**' relates to both your living family, especially your parents and your blood relations, and your ancestors. It is also concerned with your company or corporation if you are an employee, as well as all the other 'tribes' to which you belong:

e.g. if you are a cyclist, you belong to the 'tribe' of cyclists
if you are a martial artist, you belong to the 'tribe' of martial artists
if you are a builder, you belong to the 'tribe' of builders

as well as your neighbors, who are part of your local 'tribe'.

'**Windfall Profits**' relates to large sums of money such as, lottery wins, inheritances and large bonus payments.

'**Health**' relates to your health on all levels, spiritual, mental, emotional and physical.

'**Heaven/Helpful People**' relates to cash flow, travel, helpful people and everything to do with flow in your life. Helpful people may be friends but not necessarily. In this case, '**Helpful People**' means anyone who is paid to provide you with a service. For example a builder, plumber or mechanic.

'**Offspring/Creativity**' relates to your own children, and also to any of your creative endeavours. i.e. the children of your mind.

Producing and directing a play, writing a book or a song, and painting a picture are all examples of creative projects that are ruled by these areas.

It is very important, if you choose to emphasize 'Offspring/Creativity', that you are aware that you are enhancing creativity on **all** levels. This means your physical fertility!

Make sure your contraception is good, as well as consistent, if you enhance these areas, and do NOT want to be a parent right now!

Likewise, if you want to have children, these are wonderful areas to enhance to support your plans to conceive.

'Transformation/Knowledge' is about your relationship with yourself, and is also to do with knowledge and studies. It is called 'Transformation' because radical change usually only takes place because of additional specialist knowledge.

Some people regard this as an area that relates to spiritual practice, i.e. meditation. You can also think of this area as being about you talking to the Universe.

This is a key area for anyone in crisis.

'Fame/Illumination' is about your reputation, and how you are seen by others. It is also about those 'ah ha' moments, when suddenly the penny drops, and the solution becomes obvious.

It also relates to spiritual practice. While **'Transformation/Knowledge'** is about you talking to the Universe, **'Fame/Illumination'** is about the Universe talking back to you.

THE COMPASS SECTORS AND HOW TO USE THE 8 DIRECTIONS

As well as looking at the sectors of the Bagua, it is useful to look at the compass sectors as well. This form of feng shui is called the 'Compass School'.

In practice, the best results come from combining both methods.

With the compass method of feng shui, the first thing to do is find the geometric center of your home. Please refer to Chapter 4 for more detailed instructions about this.

It is extremely important that this information is accurate.

Each of the 8 compass directions relates to a specific life sector, while the center of the space relates to health.

This central space has the same significance for both the Compass and the 3 Gate Method of Chi schools of feng shui.

You will notice that in feng shui books, the compass is always shown reversed. This is a Chinese convention. North is still North and South is still South. It is just a different way of writing things.

COMPASS DIRECTIONS AND THEIR RELATIONSHIPS TO THE LIFE SECTORS

North	'Career'
South West	'Relationships/Marriage'
East	'Family/Elders'
South East	'Windfall Profits'
Center	'Health'
North West	'Heaven/Helpful People'
West	'Offspring/Creativity'
North East	'Transformation/Knowledge'
South	'Fame/Illumination'

CREATING FLOW

Cash Flow, Helpful People and the North West

The importance of recycling

'Cash Flow' and 'Helpful People', as well as relating to the bottom right sector of the Bagua, are also concerned with the **North West** sector of your home/office.

The interesting thing about any cash, or money that you have, is that it has all been given to you by somebody else. Maybe you have earned it, maybe you won it, and maybe some of it came to you as a gift.

It is all part of a bigger circulation. As a form of exchange, money is so useful that if we didn't have it someone would have to invent it!

An easy way to activate 'flow' in your life is to recycle on a very consistent basis.

This involves more than just separating your trash into paper/cardboard/metal and plastic.

It means that if someone offers you something, you accept it. If you do not want it yourself, you immediately pass it on. By doing this, you are creating 'flow'.

It does not matter whether you give it to a charity shop, or to a friend, or you sell it. The important thing here is that the item moves, and that you are instrumental in creating this flow.

Another easy way to activate flow in your life is to give to charity. By doing this, the message you send to your own unconscious mind is that you already have more than enough. Remember 'like attracts like'.

HOW TO ENHANCE THESE AREAS

Apart from ensuring these areas are clean, clear and uncluttered, adding the following objects will energize these sectors:

A MIRROR OR MIRRORS

Ensure that each mirror reflects something beautiful, and there is also artwork on the wall behind the mirror.

If this wall is a party wall, you will be emphasizing your neighbor's influence in your life. Provided you get on well, this is fine. If you have any problems with your neighbors, make sure there are NO mirrors on any party walls with them.

If the area behind the mirror is on an outside wall, this has the effect of bringing the outside in. Obviously in this case, it depends what is outside, and whether you want to bring it inside!

People very often hang a mirror to reflect a well-loved garden, as this brings another area of beauty into the house.

MIRRORS TO AVOID

- Mirrored tiles because they split your image and, as such, are considered unhelpful in terms of feng shui.

- 2 mirrors directly opposite one another create what is called 'war of the mirrors'. The light is trapped, bouncing backwards and forwards in an endless loop.

  This signifies areas in your life where it appears to be impossible to make progress. Avoid this at all costs.

- Mirrors in the Shar Chi area for the year because they magnify outside interference in your life. Please see Chapter 4 to find out what the Shar Chi area is for the current year.

- A large mirror on the outside of a bathroom door, or a wall on the outside of a bathroom. This magnifies the energy of the bathroom. It is better dispersed.

- Magnifying the energy of your bathroom has unfortunate implications for your finances! Don't go there!

- A mirror directly opposite the toilet, i.e. in a position that reflects you sitting on it.

  In every home that I have visited with this formation, there have been serious money problems, with losses running into thousands of dollars.

- Any mirrors in an office space. The reason for this is that the mirror has the effect of doubling the paperwork, but not the profits!

MORE ENERGY ENHANCERS

Lights

An electric light or candle that is lit for 3 hours a day, as an absolute minimum, will act as an enhancement.

Artwork

Pictures that relate to movement, travel, groups of people working together harmoniously and round, circular objects are all enhancements for the **'Heaven/Helpful People'** and the **North West** sectors.

Also useful are pictures of market places, where exchanges and trades are happening.

Pictures of bridges are especially good, as they symbolize having access to 2 areas easily. They are helpful during times of major change.

The closer you can get to a physical representation of what you would like to manifest, the better the art work will function as a feng shui cure.

Round or spherical, shiny metallic objects

As the 'Heaven/Helpful People' area is ruled by the element or **Metal**, all metal objects act as enhancements here, especially round ones – the spherical shape symbolizing flow and movement.

You can use a round metal tray, a metal vase with a spherical shape, or a metal ball as 'cures' for these areas. Even coins would be appropriate.

Round glass faceted crystal balls

A crystal ball hanging in a window throws rainbows.

Symbolically, and, especially in the Western world, a rainbow signifies happiness and the pot of gold at the end of it. Multiple rainbows are excellent!

Simple 5 element cure or installation

This involves putting all 5 elements in one place. This is easily done by assembling the following:

a clear or cut crystal glass bowl	
with a layer of semi-precious stones on the bottom	EARTH
a layer of coins on top of them	METAL
covered by water exposed to sunlight for 3 hours	WATER
with petals or floating flowers on top of the water	WOOD
with a floating candle or tea light lit for 3 hours a day	FIRE

Change the water and the petals every few days, and the candle daily.

'FORTUNATE BLESSING' /'WINDFALL PROFITS' AND THE SOUTH EAST

The attitude of gratitude

'Fortunate Blessings'/Windfall Profits' relates to the upper left hand corner of the Bagua, and to the South East sector of your home/office.

The easiest way to activate this type of energy in your life is to have an 'attitude of gratitude'. In other words, you continually notice all the things, situations and people in your life for whom you are grateful. The more you do this, the more you attract **'Fortunate Blessings'**.

How to add energy to the 'Fortunate Blessings/Windfall Profits' and the South East areas

Some of the same things that work as enhancements in the **'Heaven'** and **'Helpful People'** areas are also useful in these areas.

NB This area is ruled by the element of **Wood** and so it is not helpful to put metal objects in this area, as **Metal** controls or 'kills' **Wood**, according to the 5 Element Control Cycle.

All of the following will do the same job of adding energy:

a mirror or mirrors
a round glass faceted crystal ball
lights
simple 5 element cure or installation

In the **'Fortunate Blessings/Windfall Profits'** and **South East**, lights and plants are absolutely crucial. The following are also very helpful –

Artwork

Pictures that relate to abundance in any way that is meaningful to you

Pictures of people eating

Pictures of people in sumptuous surroundings

Pictures of harvests, fruit, flowers and trees

Pictures of a ship/ships

Pictures of bridges

Pictures of markets

Lights and Plants

The **'Fortunate Blessings'** area is greatly enhanced by at least one light and at least one plant. The brighter the light and the larger the plant, the better!

I would strongly urge you to ensure that you have at least a light and a plant in both the **'Fortunate Blessings'** and the **South East** sectors of your home/office.

FENG SHUI TIPS FOR CONSERVING WEALTH

Bathroom corrections

As the element of **Water** is symbolic of money in feng shui, doing bathroom corrections is considered helpful in terms of conserving money. These are general bathroom corrections:

1. Keep the plugs in, in the sink, bath, and shower

2. Keep the lid of the toilet down

3. Have as many green plants and/or green objects in the area as possible

4. Place some red/hot pink objects in there, unless the bathroom falls in the Shar Chi area for the year

5. Place a small round convex mirror on the outside of the bathroom door at the throat height of the tallest person in the house

Corrections for stairs

Stairs are considered to be 'up and down energy'. This is symbolic of instability – less than desirable, especially where finances are concerned.

It is usually a good idea to correct for this by putting a heavy object, such as a bookcase, around the stairs, where possible. When this is impractical, artwork of mountains and/or large rocks will do.

Frequently, the entrance to an apartment or home is at the bottom of a flight of stairs.

In this situation, place a mirror with art work opposite it, to stop the energy symbolically rolling out of the front door. Where this is not possible, perhaps because this area falls in the Shar Chi area for the year, use a 6 hollow tubed metal wind chime instead.

In some staircases, the stair treads are open at the back. This is often true for fire escapes and spiral stair cases. The feng shui cure, in this instance, is to close off the area at the back of the each stair tread.

It is usually possible to do this when the stairs concerned are in your own home. You can use metal, wood or plastic (or even fabric, as a temporary measure) to close them off.

Fire escape stair cases are another story. As there are stringent regulations applying to them, just bless them, as this almost certainly will be an area that falls outside of your direct control.

Fences and boundaries

As well as being important for relationships, good boundaries symbolize the ability to control your resources. These are excellent reasons to make sure all your fences are in order, and that your gates and doors shut properly and lock where appropriate.

Manhole covers

This again relates to the element of **Water**.

The very best cure here is to replace the man-hole cover with a recessed one. This allows you to fill the man-hole cover with a layer of earth and plant it out with something like camomile, or any resilient plant which easily survives being walked over.

Less expensive and easier cures are:

- to paint the man-hole cover either green or red

- to place a green mat over the man-hole cover with a heavy terracotta pot, nicely planted out on top of it.

If this man-hole cover falls in the Shar Chi area for the year, use a green pot and paint the man-hole cover green. Avoid red or orange flowers here.

IMPORTANT CONSIDERATIONS FOR OFFICES

A distant view

When you sit at your desk, you should be able to see out into the distance, preferably out of a window.

If there are no windows in your office, ensure that you have distant view art work on the wall opposite you, so that you have a sense of space.

Good seating

A high backed chair, that is fully adjustable with 5 feet, gives support for your back, and should be comfortable. The longer your working day, the more important this is – along with good positioning of your computer and keyboard.

Ideally, the height of your chair is such that your feet rest on the ground, and the angle of your knees and feet to your hips makes a right angle.

The height of your desk is arranged so that the bend of your arms makes a right angle.

Investing in a vertical mouse, if you spend long hours at your computer, helps to prevent repetitive strain injury, also known as RSI.

Your computer screen or laptop ideally is positioned so that, either you are looking up at 15° angle or straight ahead.

Adding a small rolled towel to the curve in your low back can also help to make your sitting position a very comfortable one.

Wherever possible, sit with a wall behind you, and a good view of the door. This symbolizes support and protection – very important if you are running a company or managing a department.

Keep heavy items stored on the ground, or on lower level shelves. Avoid having large files on overhead shelves. Doing this will give you more of a feeling of space and openness.

Keep your paperwork in several small stacks, rather than one large one. Psychologically, it then appears that you have fewer tasks waiting, and your resistance to doing them is therefore reduced.

As mentioned before, do not hang mirrors in an office space. Why would you want to double your paperwork, but not the profits?

Happiness – The by-product of a balanced life

" I'll paint rainbows all over your blues "

John Sebastian, The Lovin' Spoonful

Chapter 7
Happiness – The by-product of a balanced life

Although the 'pursuit of happiness' is a right under the US constitution, pursuing it is generally not the way forward!

One of the ways of experiencing this most desirable of states is to have the following 4 components of your life in a good balance with each other.

These 4 components are:

Health, Love, Work, Self Expression

A lack of any 1 of these 4 components makes it more of a challenge to experience happiness. The presence of all 4 makes just makes it easier.

Here are some other interesting definitions of happiness:

According to the Science of Happiness website, people who experience happiness pay attention to all the following 7 areas of their lives:

Relationships
Caring
Exercise
Flow
Spiritual Engagement and Meaning
Strengths and Virtues
Positive Thinking: Optimism and Gratitude

"Thousands of candles can be lighted from a single candle, and the life of the candle will not be shortened. Happiness never decreases by being shared."
Buddha

"The greatest degree of inner tranquility comes from the development of love and compassion. The more we care for the happiness of others, the greater is our own sense of well-being."
Tenzin Gyatso, 14th Dalai Lama

"Most people are about as happy as they make up their minds to be."
Abraham Lincoln

"People say that money is not the key to happiness, but I always figured if you have enough money, you can have a key made."
Joan Rivers

FLOW

Whatever your definition of happiness, most people will agree that they feel best when they are in 'their flow'.

In this state, time ceases to exist and we are engrossed in something that takes us outside of ourselves.

In feng shui terms, the flow of energy through your home symbolizes the flow of energy through your life.

Maximize your 'flow' by ensuring that all the hallways, corridors, stairs and entrances to rooms are clear and uncluttered. All the doors should open and close easily and the same applies for all the windows.

Every so often, it is a good idea to open all the windows and all the doors of your home to literally 'clear the air'.

THE FRONT DOOR

The most important door in feng shui terms is your front door. Ideally the path up to it will be curving rather than just a straight line. Remember Shar Chi is able to rush in along straight lines. You are trying to encourage a gentle even flow of energy.

A BLESSING ON YOUR HOME

In many cultures and religions there is a specific item placed near the front door or over it as a symbol of protection of the home.

In Turkey, this will be the Nazar Boncuğu, which protects against the evil eye.

In Jewish culture, there is the Mezuzah – a small scroll with writing from the Talmud attached to the door post.

In Hindu culture, depending on your preferences, it can be a statue or picture of Ganesh, the Elephant God of Wisdom.

In Muslim culture, the Hamsa or 'Hand of Fatima' is the symbol of protection.

For Christians, it is The Cross.

Devout Buddhists set up an altar with the likeness of The Buddha and sometimes dedicate a whole room as a shrine.

In China, many households will have a Bagua mirror over, or on their front door. I strongly counsel Westerners against doing this, as it usually just makes your front door look strange to neighbors and passers-by.

The purpose of a Bagua mirror is to deflect outside energies away from your home. You can easily do this by using the more usual Western symbol of a nice shiny brass or metallic door knocker.

This has the advantage of being in harmony with your neighborhood and culture, and has no religious connotations. It is, therefore, ideal for anyone.

DOORS IN GENERAL

Doors symbolize opportunities. They should be positioned in such a way that they do not crash against each other when they open.

Be aware that if you reflect any particular door in a mirror, you will be emphasizing the room, and the person who occupies the room behind that door.

This is especially relevant if you magnify the door of one child. You may well find that this little person is having a greater say in the running of the household than perhaps you would like.

If you are single, ideally you will not have any mirrors in your bedroom. However, if you do have a mirror in your bedroom that reflects your door, the probability of you having a series of one night stands increases dramatically.

The mirror is, in effect, magnifying the 'way out'. In other words, someone comes in, and then they leave.

If you reflect stairs in a mirror, be aware that you are reflecting an energy of instability.

If you do have a mirror around your stairs, hang it so that it does not reflect the stairs. Make sure you have some mountain art work as a counter-balance to the stairs in this area.

The correction for stairs coming down directly opposite the front door is a mirror just inside the doorway, to the left or right of the stairs, but not reflecting them.

(This is always dependant on whether this is the Shar Chi area for the year or not. If it is the Shar Chi area, then remove the mirror, and hang a 6 hollow-tubed metal wind chime over the doorway).

Also, ensure that this mirror reflects some artwork, preferably of something uplifting.

Remember if you magnify a blank wall, you are magnifying nothing!

$$0 \times 0 = 0$$

Anything multiplied by 0 = 0

If you have a mirror directly opposite your front door, you will encourage the members of the household to spend most of their time away from home.

BALANCE

The most basic energetic balance is that of **Yin** and **Yang** – the male/female balance. It is, however, also more than that. Here follows a list of 'Yin' qualities with their balancing 'Yang' qualities opposite.

Yin	Yang
Female	Male
Soft	Hard
Yielding	Firm
Dark	Light
Negative	Positive
Moonlight	Sunlight
Water	Fire
Earth	Heaven
Cold	Hot

To give some practical examples of creating balance, consider 2 women living together, whether they are sisters, mother and daughter, friends, or in a lesbian relationship.

This situation is one where there is double Yin energy. This pair need to ensure that they have a bit of extra Yang energy in their surroundings to make the balance. This could mean having more candles, fires (both real and/or electric), large heavy items and brightly colored objects around them.

What about 2 men living together? They could be 2 brothers, a father and son, friends, cousins or gay lovers. In all of these situations, there is double Yang energy and so to make the balance, it is extremely important to make sure there is some extra Yin energy to compensate.

This could take the form of more soft furnishings such as curtains, rugs, table cloths and cushions. House plants will also soften the Chi, as will pets – cats, dogs or fish. A water feature also supplies the necessary Yin energy, as do black, blue and dark colored objects.

Teenage boys very frequently choose an all black room. This is because they are at their most Yang physically. A black room provides the dark, womb-like Yin surroundings that balance them out.

Relax mothers and fathers! This is a temporary situation and you will probably find that as soon as your son has a girlfriend, he will want to paint his room a different color.

In terms of balance, the overall climate of where you live is also very important.

Cool marble, white walls and blue and green interiors, all of which are Yin, work very well in hot climates.

They supply the Yin energy necessary to balance the heat and strong sunlight there. They tend to work less well in colder climates, as what is needed there is the element of **Fire** to balance out the rain and snow.

FIRE AND WATER – YOUR PURPOSE AND INSPIRATION

Going back to happiness being the by-product of a balanced life, a very key balance in terms of feng shui and the Bagua is that of **Fire** and **Water**, extreme Yang and extreme Yin.

This balance symbolizes the human journey of man through life to find 'Illumination' or enlightenment. In this instance, **Water** represents a person's purpose and **Fire** represents enlightenment.

Every time you have one of those 'ah ha' moments, you are experiencing a mini form of enlightenment – literally the 'lights go on'.

The interaction of the elements of **Fire** and **Water** is somewhat violent and extreme – producing steam. Balance this by interposing the element of **Wood** between them.

Nowhere is this more important than in the kitchen. Both **Fire** and **Water** are essential. Every kitchen needs a cooker and a sink. The ideal placement of **Fire** and **Water** in a kitchen is in a triangular formation with the refrigerator.

However, if **Fire** and **Water** are directly opposite each other in the kitchen, it symbolizes husband and wife fighting. In the West, this is considered to be a divorce formation.

If you move into a house or apartment with this configuration, it is the first thing that needs changing to protect the future of your romantic relationship.

On the plus side, although the combination of **Fire** and **Water** is a volatile one, it is also highly creative! This is why your hot water boiler for your central heating, being a working combination of **Fire** and **Water**, is considered to be a triple plus wherever it falls.

YOUR LIVING ROOM – THE SYMBOL OF HOW YOU LIVE YOUR LIFE

To balance this important room, do all of the following:

- light all 4 corners of the room

- have a large green plant in the far left corner and/or the South East sector of this room

- display family pictures and pictures both of, and by your children in this area

- arrange the seating around a fire place, rather than the TV, if at all humanly possible

Needless to say, the absolute basics are that this room is clean, clear and uncluttered!

While we are on the subject of balance...

HOW DO YOU BALANCE YOUR SPACE IF YOUR HOME IS NOT AN EVEN SQUARE OR RECTANGLE?

If, when you draw the footprint or floor plan of your home, it is not an even square or rectangle, you will either have 'missing space' or an addition.

WHAT IS MISSING SPACE?

This is the gap in the rectangle or square formation of your home's footprint.

Wherever this occurs on your floor plan, you are likely to find that you have 'potential' for what this area represents, as well as being challenged by it.

This is frequently the case in terms of money, when the back left-hand corner of the property has missing space. This area corresponds to what is called **'Fortunate Blessings'** or **'Windfall Profits'** on the Bagua.

While some people are able to build an extension in this area to compensate, many of us need to find other, less costly ways around this.

The feng shui advice for people adding an extension to the back of their home is to extend the entire building line, so as to avoid creating missing space.

The reason is that if you create missing space in the far left-hand corner (standing at your front door looking into the house) you are negatively influencing your **'Fortunate Blessings'** or **'Windfall Profits'** area.

If you create missing space in the far right-hand corner (standing at your front door looking into the house), you are negatively influencing your **'Relationships/Marriage'** area.

This is why it is better to extend the entire building line. Nothing too important here, just your money and your love life!

Please refer to page 32 for some examples of floor plans with missing space.

CORRECTING FOR MISSING SPACE: GENERAL

It is ALWAYS important to correct for missing space. Here is how you do it:

If there is a window along the wall adjacent to the missing space, hang a small round glass faceted crystal ball in the window.

If one of the adjacent walls has no windows, hang a large mirror on this wall. Only do this if this wall does not fall in the Shar Chi area for the year.

I would also caution you against hanging a mirror in your bedroom if you are looking for love, and, especially if you already have a partner.

The reason for this is that a mirror in your bedroom has the effect of interposing someone, or something, between you and your mate. This could be work, your in-laws, a relative, a child or children, or, worst-case scenario, another lover.

Whenever you hang a mirror, make sure that it reflects something beautiful, and preferably something that you aspire to, or that has a positive meaning for you. Mirrors act as magnifiers.

Remember, if you magnify a blank wall, you magnify nothing, which gives you nothing. i.e. $0 \times 0 = 0$!

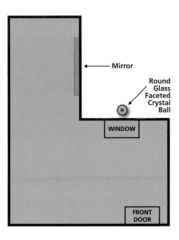

Mirror

Round Glass Faceted Crystal Ball

WINDOW

FRONT DOOR

If one of the walls adjacent to the missing space falls in the Shar Chi area, and it has a window, hang a 6 hollow-tubed metal wind chime in this window.

When you hang this wind chime, it is extremely important to make sure that you do not have a mirror in the room and/or a round glass faceted crystal ball hanging in another window in the same room.

In this case, use a large, green plant with round leaves, instead of the wind chime.

The reason for this is that wind chimes disperse, and mirrors and round glass faceted crystal balls magnify. Feng shui is about balancing energy, and if you put a 'magnifier' in a room with a 'disperser', the end result will be a lot of work that produces nothing.

The easiest cure to make occurs when your missing space is outside. If the missing space is a garden or patio area, ensure that it is beautiful. Also ensure that there is at least one large luxurious plant there, and at least one light.

Use this space as much as possible, and define it with garden furniture, and/or pots and rocks.

If the garden space contains a drain cover, you will need to correct for this. Let us assume that this manhole cover falls in an area which is not a thoroughfare.

In this case, the correction is easily made by placing a red or green mat over the manhole cover, and placing a large nicely planted out pot on top of it.

If the drain cover falls in an area that is a thoroughfare, you can paint it either green or red.

The best correction of all is to substitute the cover for a recessed manhole cover, which can be planted out with something like camomile. This particular plant is resilient in terms of being stepped on, and provides the necessary **Wood** energy.

If you are unable to hang mirrors, or round glass faceted crystal balls to make the correction, you can also enhance each area of the missing space in all the other rooms of your home where it is actually present.

Just as a reminder, the energy enhancers are:

a mirror or mirrors
a round glass faceted crystal ball
lights
simple 5 element cure or installation

CORRECTING FOR MISSING AREAS: COMPASS DIRECTION

If you have missing space, as well a missing area of the Bagua, you will also have a missing area in at least one compass direction. This can be quite important if the missing compass area happens to be one of your good directions.

Doing the corrections for missing space on the Bagua will have a positive effect.

If the missing area is in your **'Breath of Prosperity'** direction, put enhancements in this compass sector in each of the major rooms of your house/apartment, i.e. the bedroom, living room and kitchen areas.

Add the **Water** element, which enhances this direction, as either perfume, water, oils or wine and blue and/or black colored objects.

The same technique can be used for your other 3 good compass directions, taking care to add the relevant elements for the specific directions.

Please see Chapter 10 for more details.

Here is an example of a home with missing space in the West.

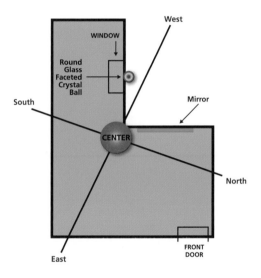

EXAMPLES OF CORRECTIONS IF YOUR 'BREATH OF PROSPERITY' DIRECTION FALLS IN 'MISSING SPACE'

Let us say, for example, that your Kua number is 6 and your **'Breath of Prosperity'** direction is West.

Should you have missing space in the West, besides the general corrections for missing space given above, please do the following:

Stand in the center of your living room, and take a compass reading to find the Western sector of this room. The enhancements for the **'Breath of Prosperity'** direction are water, liquids and blue and black colored objects.

Therefore, make sure that you have some or all of these in the West.

Repeat the same process for the kitchen, bedroom and the bathroom areas.

Another variant on this is to put an "installation" in the Western sectors of the major rooms of the house.

MAKING AN INSTALLATION

An installation contains all 5 elements:

Use a clear glass bowl filled with

■ water exposed to sunlight	**Water**
OR spring water OR filtered water	
■ a layer of semi precious stones	**Earth** covered by
■ a layer of coins	**Metal** and
■ petals or a flower/flowers	**Wood** and
■ at least one tea light or floating candle	**Fire**

Change the water and the petals every few days.

Lighting the candle for 3 hours a day activates the installation.

ADDITIONAL SPACE

It may be that, instead of missing space, you have extra space in certain areas. How can you tell which is which?

It is considered to be additional space, when one of the building lines is less than ½ of the footprint of your home. For examples please see below.

Additional space in any of the areas is considered to be a positive influence, and counts as a 'plus' for that sector.

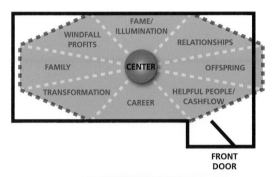

Additional space in "Cashflow/Helpful People"

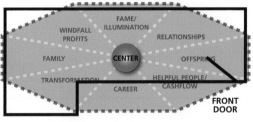

Additional space in "Transformation/ Knowledge"

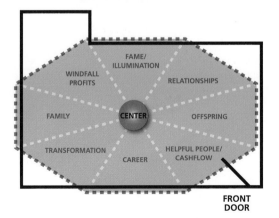

Additional space in "Windfall Profits/ Fortunate Blessings"

Harmony

" Ebony and ivory live together in perfect harmony

Side by side on my piano keyboard, oh lord why don't we? "

Paul McCartney

Chapter 8
Harmony

DEFINITION

Pleasing arrangement of parts – lack of conflict

Feng shui is based on the Eastern idea of harmony, which is about the balance of the Yin (feminine) energies and the Yang (masculine) energies.

It also relates to the Chinese book of wisdom called the I Ching, also known as the Yi Jing.

Yi means 'change' and Jing means 'book, classic'.

The literal translation of its name is 'change book', more eloquently expressed as 'Book of Changes'.

The I Ching is a 5,000 year old oracle. Its central idea is that the only thing that is certain in life is change. If you are going to have to go through it, it may as well be easy!

The idea is to find balance and harmony within change as far as possible. By and large, the book is not judgemental.

All oracles work on the principle of foretelling the future by reading the signs in the present. This is the basis of **ALL** forms of divination.

At any point, a human being can exercise his or her free will, and make a decision which changes the pattern of events, and literally alters the flow of time.

The reason oracles work is that we are creatures of habit, and often resist change, unless, and until, it is thrust upon us.

If you want to create balance and harmony in the future, it is most easily done by being focused on balance and harmony in the present, with an eye to the future.

Remember, feng shui is about both time and space.

There is a dynamic balance between your external harmony, i.e. your surroundings and your internal harmony, i.e. how you feel on the inside.

As we are 3 dimensional beings, in our world, time is always relevant.

Your home is already right, just as it is. It is a reflection of where you have arrived, and your own personal balance in the here and now.

Focusing on and honoring the present moment allows you to accept your surroundings as they are, while you bring about the changes that you want to create.

It is really important that they add beauty, enjoyment and ease for you and your family. If you like them, they are right. If you don't, they are not.

IT IS THE THOUGHT THAT COUNTS!

Your good intentions are paramount.

"Blow away the dust, now come to the living water"
from the Tao Te Ching translated by Jay Ramsay

There is an old story about a feng shui master who was travelling through a remote rural area on his way home. He had run out of water the previous day. It was a hot day and he was tired and desperate for a drink.

He saw a woman and her three sons working in the fields nearby and hurried towards them and asked for some water.

The woman obliged, and poured some of her water into a bowl. Then, she threw some chaff into the water, and handed it to him.

He was at first delighted to be offered the water, and then incensed, because she had 'polluted' the water. He couldn't gulp it down because he had to keep blowing the chaff on the surface out of the way.

"I'll get you," he thought to himself.

They started chatting and she mentioned that she was a widow with three sons to support.

He then said to her, "I know just the place for you. There is an empty house in the valley I have just come from, which would be ideal for you and your sons. Maybe you should check it out.".

The woman thanked him, and he bade her good day, and carried on his journey.

Some years later, he had reason to be in the same area again, and as he passed down the same road, the woman he had previously met called to him from the fields, and came over to speak to him.

She thanked him profusely. "Thank you so much sir, for your excellent advice. My sons and I have prospered beyond anything I could have imagined when I met you. I cannot thank you enough."

"How can this be?" said the feng shui master. "I sent you to the worst house imaginable!"

"Why would you do that sir? How could I have offended you, on such a short acquaintance?"

"You threw chaff on the water you offered me to drink" said the feng shui master.

"It was a very hot day, and I could see that you were tired and thirsty. I threw the chaff on the water so that you would have to drink it slowly, rather than gulping it down – which I knew would have made you uncomfortable".

"Madam, I have cursed you and every day Heaven blesses you. Please forgive my ignorance." The feng shui master went on his way.

GOOD RELATIONSHIPS STARTING WITH THE RELATIONSHIP YOU HAVE WITH YOURSELF

In terms of relationships, there are 2 areas of the Bagua that are important. The obvious one is the **'Relationship'** or **'Marriage'** area and the less obvious one is the **'Transformation/Knowledge'**, also known as **'Mountain'** area of the Bagua.

In ancient China, hermits went up into the mountains to meditate and do spiritual practice, away from other people and the hustle and bustle of life.

In our modern day existence, we do not usually have the luxury of just taking off for the mountains! However, there is always the mountain within you. The more challenging your life, and the more people you interact with, the more important it is to spend time alone with yourself quietly reflecting and, if possible, meditating.

Half an hour a day alone in nature – this could be walking in a park – is usually enough to bring a sense of balance and calm to the busiest of lives.

Interestingly, walking the dog has proven to be more successful than going to the gym, in terms of getting fit long-term. If you are able to have some quiet time alone while doing this, so much the better.

TRANSFORMATION AND THE NORTH EAST

The **'Transformation/Knowledge'** area of the Bagua and the North East compass sector of your home are about your relationship with yourself. These areas also signify anything to do with study, knowledge, wisdom and academic success.

You can understand why this area is also called **'Transformation'** when you consider that often, to make really positive dramatic changes, money may not be enough or even relevant. It is knowledge and wisdom that have the potential to completely turn things around 180°.

"Know thyself" is very ancient advice.

It is engraved on the walls of the temple at Delphi, home of the Oracle, a thousand years before the birth of Christ.

This phrase was repeated by Socrates, another Greek, who died in 399 BC.

Alexander Pope, who lived between 1688 and 1744, wrote the following lines in his poem called 'Know Thyself':

"Know then thyself, presume not God to scan;
The proper study of mankind is Man".

The aim here is to know and balance all parts of oneself.

MIRRORED TILES

For you to have a good relationship with yourself you need to feel whole and integrated. For this reason, mirrored tiles in your home or office are best avoided, as, symbolically, they are splitting your image into a number of smaller ones.

If they do not fall in the Shar Chi area, you could paint over them. Ideally, if they are in an area where you want a mirror, replace them with one single large mirror.

GOOD BOUNDARIES MAKE GOOD NEIGHBORS AND GOOD FRIENDS

Boundary disputes are one of the most common legal issues that bring people to court. It seems we are very territorial animals.

In feng shui terms it is essential to make sure that the borders of your property are intact, with no gaps. Avoid X formations fencing and go for + instead.

The parallel situation in your life is one where your psychological boundaries are constantly being breached. Some examples of this might be:

- People in your office expecting you to take on extra work, or do extra hours, without extra pay

- Friends expecting you to give them more help than you easily can, in terms of both money and time

- People, generally, making assumptions about what you will and won't do, without consulting you first

If any of these scenarios sound familiar, then check your physical boundaries as well as your psychological ones.

Although anger has a bad reputation as far as emotions go, it does have an important function. It is to let both you and anyone else concerned know that your standards and/or boundaries have been violated in some respect.

If you fail to communicate your displeasure, you are expecting someone else to 'mind read' what is happening. There is a fine art to doing this tactfully.

Let others know what your rules are, whenever they metaphorically and/or physically cross one of your lines, as soon as possible after the event, preferably immediately.

With regard to your home, make sure that your doors shut properly, and your locks are in good working order.

By the same token, gates and doors that are never opened or used may signify opportunities that you choose to ignore.

Generally speaking, you will tend to be friends with people who have similar cultural backgrounds and/or expectations. This is because it is easier to relate to people who share your unspoken values and boundaries.

FRIENDSHIPS AND ROMANTIC RELATIONSHIPS

Boundaries are important in romantic relationships as well as friendships. Just because someone is your boyfriend, it does not mean that they are willing to spend 3 hours on a Saturday repairing your car.

Likewise, it also means that your girlfriend may be unwilling to spend 3 hours on a Wednesday night cooking dinner and entertaining the friends you have suddenly brought over.

Communication and negotiation are everything!

In terms of romantic relationships, doing feng shui in your home will keep you together, if that is your destiny. If not, and you do split up with your partner, feng shui changes in your home will ensure that the break-up is more likely to be amicable and reasonable.

There is no way that any feng shui consultant can know for certain what the outcome will be. It is simply a case of doing everything to balance and enhance the relationship areas, and waiting to see what transpires.

I have turned up to do a consultation when the couple in question were literally on the verge of splitting up that very minute! I knocked on the door. When they both opened it, I said I was there to do the feng shui consultation they had booked.

They both looked at me in utter surprise, as if I had just stepped off another planet. At that time, the husband was literally packing his bags upstairs in the bedroom.

Fortunately, they decided to go ahead with the consultation, and called a truce for the next few hours.

As we went around their home, there were things I suggested that appealed to either one or the other of them. When this happened, one would usually say to the other "There, see, I told you so."

Fortunately, the changes required appealed to each of them, in an approximately equal ratio – half and half.

I did explain to them at the time that, were they to do these changes, if they were meant to be together, then that would be the outcome. If they were meant to split up, then that would be the case. In any event, the best solution would become obvious to both of them.

Six months later they referred one of their relatives to me, and I found out that they actually stayed together.

There are other instances when I have been to a couple's home and they have stayed together for a few more months, before deciding that the best solution for each of them would be to part.

Friendships and romantic relationships fall in the **'Relationships/Marriage'** area of the Bagua, the South Western sector of your home/office and the **'Relationship'** area of the compass relating to your Kua number (please see Chapter 10 for more information on this).

To enhance your **'Relationship'** area add some or all of the following:

- Semi-precious stones and crystals
  (here we mean crystal rocks rather than cut-glass crystals)

- Paired objects

- Sculptures or artwork of human couples, a man and a woman if you are heterosexual, 2 men or 2 women if you are gay

- A light or pole, sunk into the ground in the South West of your garden

NB Very fast results are possible, if you are able to get art work that closely resembles yourself and the partner you are trying to attract, especially if this art work is opposite a mirror. For one lady, it happened within 24 hours!

The color red and candles also work as romantic cures because the element of **Fire** supports the element of **Earth**, which is the ruling element for friendships and romance.

While good feng shui can attract the right circumstances for romance, it cannot make up for poor strategy.

One of my clients was romantically involved with a married man who purportedly did not love his wife, but felt guilty about leaving her. He had been married for a very long time.

In common with many other people in this sort of scenario, this lady had a number of objects that were part of a trio, which meant there was a lot of symbolism of threesomes in her home.

She also had a mirror in the Shar Chi area in her bathroom, which was difficult to move. However, this was something she managed to do, and she changed the objects from trios to pairs. Within 6 weeks, she informed me that her lover had left his wife and moved into a studio apartment.

I did not hear from her again for another 3 months when she told me the following tale:

Shortly after her lover moved out of his marital home, she 'felt sorry' for him and the upshot was he spent 6 nights out of 7 with her.

After 2 months, the gentleman moved back into his marital home.

Anytime you spend 4 or more nights out of 7 living with your lover, you are, de facto, and certainly from an energetic standpoint, living together.

Someone who has just gone through a break-up needs a bit of time on their own, certainly more than one night a week, before they are ready to embark on a new live-in relationship.

My client did enough feng shui to create the circumstances she was seeking.

Unfortunately, she did not seek any further advice when her lover effectively moved in.

This changed the balance of the energies in the flat that had been set up specifically for her, not for her and a man. Please see Chapter 9 for more information about this.

She also failed to take into account the importance of timing and giving her lover space. Fortunately, there were no children involved in this situation.

A new romance requires some nurturing. It really is expecting an awful lot for someone to leave a long established relationship, and then be domestically, as well as romantically, involved straight away.

CLASSIC DIVORCE FORMATION TO BE AVOIDED

Instead go for something like...

Why?

Having the cooker and the sink opposite each other in the kitchen is symbolic of a **Fire/Water** conflict between the man and woman of the house. The result is likely to be arguments at the very least. If you move in to a house or apartment with this formation, the advice is to change it, the sooner the better!

Placing the element of **Wood** between **Fire** and **Water** can sometimes help, but may not be enough. Possible cures for this situation are:

- a green mat between the cooker and the sink

- wooden flooring between the appliances

- a wooden cover for the hob and/or the sink

- a hanging basket with plants – assuming that you have a ceiling that is high enough

- hanging a small wooden wind chime between the 2 appliances – again, assuming your ceiling is high enough

MIRRORS IN THE BEDROOM

The feng shui advice is to avoid having mirrors in the bedroom, if you are in a couple relationship, and/or if you are looking to attract one. The reason for this is that the mirror is considered to magnify the space between the couple. This means that something else comes between them. This can be:

- Another lover

- A child or children

- In-laws

- Relatives

- Work

- General circumstances

One of my clients had just had a beautiful, stage-type mirror with the requisite light bulbs all around it installed in her bedroom, directly opposite her bed. When I asked her to remove it, she was most upset.

After going to a particularly interesting lecture where the subject of mirrors in bedrooms came up, I phoned this lady and said that the mirror would have to go.

Her stated objective was to attract a romantic relationship and have a child, and she had, in the last few months, met a new man.

3 weeks later she wanted to talk to me urgently, and told me what had happened after she removed the mirror.

As she was in her mid-forties, her biological clock was ticking, and she had actually broached the subject of children with her boyfriend. To her utter amazement, he replied "Darling, if you would like a baby, that's absolutely fine with me".

She was quite stunned. Over the next couple of days, as she somewhat recovered her composure, she thought long and hard about what she really wanted.

When she thought about it, she realized that, as she was doing all the work in the relationship, she didn't want a baby at that time. She didn't think that the relationship was good enough to support the arrival of a child, and communicated this to her boyfriend.

This conversation had the effect of clearing the air between them, and they did subsequently go on to have a gorgeous baby.

In this instance, it was the thought of a child that was actually coming between them as a couple. Once the mirror went, they were able to resolve things.

THE GARDEN

Your garden, if you have one, is generally considered female, and is ruled by the **Earth** element. Because of this, this area also relates strongly to friendships and romance.

With a bit of care and attention, it is possible to create a beautiful garden with only a small amount of money. Even if the soil in your garden is not of the best quality, you can always create a Zen rock garden, and have plants in tubs and pots.

MALE AND FEMALE AREAS OF THE HOME

The following areas of the Bagua are considered male:

- The **'Helpful People/Heaven'** area

- The **'Fortunate Blessings/Windfall Profits'** area

For a woman, these areas also relate to men coming into her life. If either of these areas is missing, especially the **'Cash Flow/Helpful People'** also known as **'Heaven'** area, it will be more difficult for her to attract a romantic relationship. It is essential to do the corrections for missing space.

The following areas of the Bagua are female:

- The **'Knowledge/Transformation'** area

- The **'Relationships area'**

For a man, these areas relate to women coming into his life. If either of these areas is missing, especially the **'Relationships/Marriage'** area, it will be more challenging for him to attract a loving relationship. Again, the corrections for missing space are crucial.

FAMILY RELATIONSHIPS – PARENTS AND CHILDREN

In the Bagua, the **'Elders'** or **'Tribe'** area relates to parents and relatives and the **'Offspring/Creativity'** area relates to children.

In Compass School feng shui, the Eastern sector of your home/apartment relates to parents, relatives and ancestors and the West relates to children.

The Elders area and the East are ruled by the element of **Wood**, so plants and flowers are the perfect enhancements, as well as lights and mirrors (assuming that this is not the Shar Chi area for the year!).

CHILDREN AND PETS

The **'Offspring/Creativity'** specifically relates to children and also pets. This includes cats, dogs, horses, goldfish, birds, pet snakes, tortoises, rabbits, guinea pigs, hamsters and pet mice – in fact, any living creature in your home that you or your children consider to be a pet.

In compass school feng shui, the West of your home is specifically concerned with your children and animals.

The element of **Metal** rules these subjects and any metal objects, especially round ones, act as positive energy enhancers in these areas. Bicycles and toy cars count.

TRIBES!

Besides relating to family members, the **'Elders/Tribe'** area also relates to the company you work for, and your department within it, if you work for a corporation of any kind.

It also relates to those groups of people with whom you share common interests.

For example, if you are a cyclist you belong to the tribe of cyclists. If you are a motorist you belong to the tribe of motorists. If you are a dancer, you belong to the tribe of dancers – and maybe one of the subsets of dancers, rather than just dancers in general.

It is very helpful to know which tribes you belong to, so that when you travel, or find yourself in a strange environment, your first priority is to seek out members of your own tribes.

For example if you are a vegetarian, when you visit a new city you will naturally seek out vegetarian restaurants, where it will be easy for you to meet other members of the vegetarian tribe.

Art work of people working harmoniously together is a very helpful enhancement in the **'Family/Elders'** area and the East.

Unless you live in the desert, please avoid cacti altogether, especially in these areas, as their spikes symbolize 'thorny' relationships.

All plants with round leaves are wonderful feng shui cures for the **'Family/ Elders'** area and the East.

Particular and Special Circumstances

" Life is what happens to you while you're busy making other plans. "

John Lennon
Oct 9, 1940 – Dec 8, 1980

Chapter 9
Particular and Special Circumstances

RENOVATING YOUR HOME

Remembering that feng shui is about both space and time. Every Chinese year, there are compass sectors, which are best left undisturbed. This means that you avoid doing renovations or construction work in this sector for 1 year.

These sectors are:

2012	East South East	South
2013	South South East	East
2014	South	North
2015	South South West	West
2016	West South West	South
2017	West	East
2018	West North West	North
2019	North North West	West
2020	North	South

TOTAL REFURBISHMENT!

If you are involved in the total refurbishment of a house or an apartment, it will not make sound economic sense to avoid working in certain compass sectors.

In this instance, best practice is to have a short blessing ceremony for the house or apartment. Make attendance optional for anyone concerned, and schedule it during working hours.

In multi-cultural places like Hawaii, it is quite common to have several ceremonies, including a native Hawaiian Kahuna blessing, as well as a Buddhist and a Christian one.

If you are doing the work yourself, then have a short ceremony or prayers to bless your home. You can do this yourself, or ask your local minister to conduct the service. Ask for protection during the construction work and decorating, and in future, while living there.

LIVING ON YOUR OWN

a)   In one room

If you share an apartment or house with other people – either your family, friends or fellow students – your main concern is your own room. This makes up 70% of your feng shui.

It is important to remember this, so that you keep good boundaries with your house-mates. This means that you do not expect them to take on board your feng shui beliefs and preferences.

As your personal space is also likely to be your bedroom, it is a good idea to cover any mirrors when they are not in use. This is always provided that they do not fall in the Shar Chi area for the year, as calculated from the center of your bedroom.

A long mirror on the inside of a cupboard door is a good solution again, assuming that it does not fall in the Shar Chi area for the year, of either the house or the bedroom.

If your room falls in the Shar Chi area for the house, ideally you would have no mirrors in your bedroom at all. In this case, if you must have a mirror in your room, ensure that it does not reflect your bed and do NOT cover it. Have at least one small green plant opposite it.

A small plant, provided you have good ventilation in your room, will not overly upset the oxygen balance of the air while you sleep.

The smaller the space you occupy, the greater the necessity for order becomes.

b)   In your own apartment or house

Sorting out your feng shui in this situation is relatively easy. You have only yourself to think about! You can apply both the Bagua and the compass to your space.

Start with the Bagua and remember the following:

If you are a woman living on your own, the male spaces i.e. **'Windfall Profits/Fortunate Blessings'** and the **'Heaven/Helpful People'** areas both relate to the men in your life, and men coming into your life as well as finances.

If you are a man living on your own, the female spaces i.e. **'Relationships/ Marriage'** and **'Transformation/Knowledge'** relate to the women in your life, and women coming into your life.

If you are in the happy position of having more space than you need, designate a use for each of the rooms. This dictates some basics which will make it easier to decide on furnishings, lighting and objects.

It is usually fairly easy to set up a room for 2 functions. However, as soon as you try to get a room to serve 3 functions, it becomes much more of a challenge to create a comfortable balance.

An example of this would be having a spare bedroom that doubles up as a study, OR a study that doubles up as a spare bedroom. This works fairly well provided you are not also trying to make this room into a dressing room, and/or a stock room for a business you are running on the side!

Your living room space symbolizes your living conditions generally. You need either a set-up that allows you to entertain at least one other person easily, OR transforms simply and quickly to make this possible.

This is where useful items of furniture, like fold-down tables and chairs, really make a difference.

A NEW LOVER MOVING IN

Ideally, when you decide to live together, you choose a new place together. This is often a counsel of perfection, and sometimes it is not immediately practical.

If you are involved in a long distance relationship, you may not have enough time to go house hunting together.

When anyone moves in with you, whether a lover, friend or lodger, the energetic balance of your space changes.

One of the first things that happens is that, if you are female, and a man moves in, the areas that have been your money areas now become his money areas. Your money areas now become the **'Relationship/Marriage'** sector and the **'Transformation/Knowledge'** sector.

If you are male and your girlfriend moves in, your money areas stay the same and her money areas become the **'Relationship/Marriage'** and **'Transformation/Knowledge'** areas.

This has even more implications if there is missing space in the property, as shown in the 'Missing space in Windfall Profits/Fortunate Blessings' example at the top of page 32.

For a woman, a missing **'Windfall Profits/Fortunate Blessings'** area means that her relationship area is positive, while her finances may be challenged. However, should her boyfriend move in, **'Windfall Profits/Fortunate Blessings'** would then relate to him and his money, because **'Windfall Profits'** is considered to be a male space.

If no correction is made for this missing space, it is likely that her finances will improve after he moves in, and his will become more of a challenge.

In this situation, correcting for missing space in **'Windfall Profits'** or **'Fortunate Blessings'** area helps the man improve his finances.

For the woman of the house, when living with a man, your money areas become the **'Relationship'** or **'Marriage'** space and the **'Transformation'** or **'Knowledge'** space.

For a man whose **'Relationship/Marriage'** area is missing, finding a long-term girlfriend is likely to be a challenge. Doing the feng shui adjustments for this will turn the situation around.

The other important consideration, when a new partner moves in, is to have an agreement that runs along the lines of 'everything that is visible to both is acceptable to both'.

Please refer back to Chapter 8 regarding this.

ALREADY LIVING TOGETHER AS A COUPLE

The essential considerations here involve doing the following:

- Changes for the Year
  Please see Chapter 4

- Ensure that there are no mirrors on show in your bedroom
  Please see Chapter 8

- Correct for Missing Space
  Please see Chapter 7

- Remove any objects that your lover dislikes from your shared space
  Please see Chapter 8

- Avoid positioning the sink and the cooker opposite each other (Kitchen)
  Please see Chapter 8

Each of you needs at least one area in your joint home designated as personal space. This is somewhere to keep your own items – and particularly those that your partner does not like.

The ideal agreement is that you both like whatever is in your joint space.

ALREADY LIVING TOGETHER AS A FAMILY

Anyone living in a family unit of 3 or more is already dealing with multiple relationships, e.g.

A child living with her 2 parents has the following relationships:

One with herself
One with her father
One with her mother
One with her parents as a couple

This is 3 relationships, apart from the relationship with herself!

If she has a brother, then she is involved in the following relationships:

One with herself
One with her father
One with her mother
One with her parents as a couple
One with her brother
One with her brother and her father
One with her brother and her mother and
One with her brother, her father and her mother

This is 7 relationships, other than her relationship with herself.

In these circumstances, clear boundaries – both personal ones as well as those to do with space and time – help to create family harmony.

Each family member needs some personal space, even if it is just a cupboard or a bookshelf.

BIRTH OF A NEW BABY

It will be apparent from the illustrations above, that the arrival of a new baby increases the number of relationships present for all the family members, and makes more demands of the existing space.

It is very helpful to start slowly making the changes in the household to create more space for the new baby's arrival when the mother is about 6 months pregnant. The areas to emphasize and enhance are the **'Elders/ Tribe'** area and the **'Offspring/Creativity'** area as well as the **East** and **West** sectors of your home.

For more information on this, please see Chapter 8.

INFERTILITY

Sadly, many more couples nowadays are having difficulty conceiving. Feng shui can help.

The key factors here are:

Enhancing the **'Center'** space, which relates to health
This needs to be clean, clear and uncluttered as well as well lit.

Enhancing the **'Heavenly Doctor'** compass sectors with the element of **Fire** for both man and woman as described in Chapter 5.

Correcting for missing space in **'Career'**
This relates to the element of **Water**, which is to do with conception, and also relates to the kidney meridian in acupuncture.

This is where the ancestral chi, which you pass on to your children, is held. It is like a savings account – however, an energetic one rather than a financial one. As with money, spending it is always easier than saving it.

Correcting for missing space in the **North**, again because it is **Water** ruled. This also relates to conception.

Correcting for missing space in the **'Offspring/Creativity'** area
This area relates to any existing children you may have and to children yet to be born.

Correcting for missing space in the **West**
Again, this relates to existing children and any yet to be born.

Correcting for Geopathic stress under your bed.
This relates directly to your health and that of your partner.
Please see Chapter 5, pages 69 – 71

Correcting for Vortex energy under your bed.
Again, this relates directly to your health and your partner's.
Please see Chapter 5, pages 72 – 73

DIVORCE

Doing the feng shui of your home is very useful if you are divorcing. The reason for this is that if you are meant to be together, and the situation is still retrievable, you will re-unite.

In any event, you will usually find that you gain clarity about your relationship with each other. Within a matter of weeks, it normally becomes obvious that, either you are meant to stay together, or break up.

If you are going to break up, doing feng shui in your home, usually creates an atmosphere in which it is easier for you to negotiate an amicable, or at least reasonable parting.

If you are the one staying in the marital home, and your spouse is leaving, remember that you will need to extensively space clear and redecorate your home.

If there are any obvious divorce formations, such as missing space in the 'Relationships/Marriage' area and/or a cooker and sink opposition, these will need to be corrected.

If you are leaving the home you have shared with your ex, you are in an ideal position to create a brand new home. In your situation, whether you are buying or renting, find out about the previous occupants.

If they divorced, this would be a place to avoid – unless you are able to spot an obvious formation in the kitchen or master bedroom which you can easily correct.

BUYING A NEW HOME

Ideally, as soon as you walk through the front door, you want to get the sense of being at home.

If you are in a couple relationship, and you both experience this, it is a done deal. It does not matter what adjustments you need to make. This is obviously your next home.

As a consultant, I have frequently found that people will only ask me whether they should buy a particular property when they are not really sure about it themselves.

When these same individuals find a property they love, they will ask me to do a consultation AFTER they have moved in.

If you are part of a couple, and are looking for a home together, remember that the best case scenario is one where you both like the place.

Spare your partner a sales pitch, if he/she is not of the same mind. It doesn't work anyway!

You do yourselves a big favor by avoiding this unnecessary stress. Better to hold the thought that there is somewhere out there that is perfect for both of you right now.

Apart from your own special criteria when buying a place, here are some situations to avoid, and some to seek out when you are choosing your new home:

LESS THAN DESIRABLE

- A bathroom or toilet door 180° opposite (i.e. directly opposite) the front door

- Missing space on the floor plan

- Major chronic illness of one of the family members moving out (this could indicate a greater than usual amount of geopathic stress)

- A property at the end of a cul-de-sac directly opposite the road

- A property at a T-junction directly opposite a road

- Properties adjoining grave yards

- Anything built on a flood plane – this is just common sense!

- A kitchen with the cooker/stove opposite the sink (husband and wife fight!)

- Bathroom in the center of the home

- A fountain to the right of your front door as you face out (husband has affairs)

VERY DESIRABLE

- Even shaped property – either a complete square or an octagonal building. Schizophrenics have been found to become considerably calmer in 8 sided rooms!

- Good natural light

- Good ventilation

- Decent sized hallways and corridors

- A loft (**'Heaven'** energy)

- A basement or garden (**'Earth'** energy)

- A fountain or water feature to the left of the front door as you face out

- Good predecessor chi – i.e. The people who lived in the house before were happy, had good health, and were at least OK financially

ARE YOU MOVING WITH THE ENERGY?

Another major consideration, when you are moving either home or office, is the direction in which you move. This is important because it influences your experiences over the next 12 months.

It is especially relevant when a couple start to live together for the first time. If one or both of the pair are 'moving against the energy', they will find the adaptation of living together much more difficult.

When you know about this ahead of time, you can make more allowances for your partner, if they have had to 'move against the energy' to be with you. In this instance, doing the feng shui in your new home acts as a very good counter-measure.

I have actually been to couples who have moved in together, then split up, then moved back together, because they have been unaware of this dynamic operating.

Often, the effect of moving out and then moving back together is, that instead of doing one move against the energy, one of the couple winds up doing 2 moves against the energy. Not recommended!

In these situations, the person who has 'moved against the energy' feels stressed and uncomfortable. Then they ask themselves what is different in their life. The first conclusion they come to is that the difference is living with their partner, who they then instantly blame.

The reality is that, even if they had moved on their own, they would still be feeling uncomfortable. Only there would be no-one else to blame.

The good news is that when a couple moves, usually one of them will be moving in a good direction. This is the person who needs to be organizing both moves. The partner who would be 'moving against the energy' needs to allow the other person to make all the important decisions about their move.

Who pays for things is not an issue here. Who decides the timing, the removal people, and all the details is best left to the partner with the good directions. The other person gets the greatest benefits from just going with the flow, and saying 'Yes darling'.

SELLING YOUR HOME

Apart from the issue of pricing, which is always important when selling property, here are some other key things to remember.

The first is, if you have any sort of spirit presences, your home will be much more difficult to sell. Very frequently, the occupying spirits are less than keen to share the property with human beings. An empty house suits them just fine.

Recently, a friend of mine was telling me how delighted she was that her previous house had sold quickly, while there was another property next door that had been on the market for 3 years.

When she had initially moved into her home, there were at least 2 spirit presences there. She only took the house on because she was under time constraints and desperate to move. We did everything we could to encourage them to move on.

Usually I find it is better to ask my own spirit guides to help the spirit presences go on to the next step on their journey. Not all spirits want to go to the light. Some want to go to the darkness.

Where they would like to go is not really what is at issue here. What is important is to create the conditions for them to move on, quickly and easily. To facilitate this, hold the intention, and communicate the following thoughts telepathically:

"There is help waiting for you to move on, should you wish to do so. It must be awfully boring to be in the same situation, year upon year."

Very often spirits that are earth bound fear that their actions on the earth plane have been so despicable that they will never be forgiven. This is not true. Just as there are doctors and midwives here to help new beings arrive in their physical bodies, so there are guides in the spirit realms, whose job it is to help earth bound spirits move on.

CLEARING CLUTTER AND SPACE CLEARING

When you sell your home, you are actually selling space. The easier you make it for your prospective buyers to imagine it filled with their own furniture, the more likely you are to make a sale.

Clearing your clutter out, whether by selling it, recycling it, giving it to charity or storing it, frees up more space to make this simpler.

You can also improve the energetic feel of your home:

- with a small space clearing ceremony, using bell ringing, candles and/or incense

- having a 'going away' party or a 'leaving do' which breaks up the existing energy patterns, and helps you gather your own social energy together, ready to move into your new home

MOVING HOUSE AND MOVING OFFICE

There is a great tendency, with all the many things to do when relocating either your home or your office (or both!), to decide that you will start using feng shui in your new place.

In practice it is better to make the changes in your old home/office first. When you do this, the whole process of moving becomes easier and simpler.

Even if you only get as far as clearing clutter, at least everything you start with in your new home/office will be relevant and necessary. This way, you do really leave your past behind you.

You free yourself to focus on the new people, places and experiences that will be important in your new future.

Having a leaving party is a great way of marking the end of one chapter of your life. It means that you travel on a tide of good will from your friends, family and colleagues.

A house warming party just after you arrive then grounds you and launches you on to the next phase of your life. (It also means that all your friends know where to find you at your new address.)

A Bit More Detail – Numerology

" God is in the details. "

Ludwig Mies van der Rohe
Mar 27, 1886 – Aug 17, 1969

Chapter 10
A Bit More Detail
– Numerology

You may remember, if you have been reading this book in sequence, that feng shui is about both space and time. What follows gives a little more detail about the time element of feng shui relating to the year of your birth.

For this, you will need to calculate your Kua number. This number will be different depending on whether you are male or female, and also on whether you were born in the Northern or Southern hemisphere. This means either above or below the Equator.

Each Kua number is allocated 4 good directions and 4 inauspicious directions. Please note there is no Kua number 5. If you do the calculations and arrive at 5, you are allocated Kua number 2 if you are a man, and Kua number 8 if you are a woman.

Each year, there are one or two directions that are inauspicious for everyone, irrespective of their Kua numbers. These exceptions are listed up to 2020 at the end of this chapter.

As feng shui is about creating easy change in your life, it makes sense to enhance the energies of your good directions and disperse the energies of your inauspicious directions.

Knowing your good directions, and your inauspicious ones, also helps you diagnose more precisely areas that may need adjustments to support you in creating the life that you want.

CALCULATING YOUR KUA NUMBER

First, let's look at how to calculate your Kua number.

This depends on the month and year of your birth and, some say, whether you were born in the Northern or Southern hemisphere.

As you will see Kua numbers are different for men and women. I personally think that being born in the Northern or Southern hemisphere does make a difference. I have, therefore, included the relevant calculations for those of you born in the Southern hemisphere.

My reasons for using different numbers for the Southern hemisphere are as follows:

Feng shui literally translates as 'wind water'.

The water in the Southern hemisphere rotates anti-clockwise, as opposed to clockwise in the Northern hemisphere, when in disappears down the plug hole.

Northern hemisphere movement of water

Southern hemisphere movement of water

Our planet is 70% water, and so are we humans. As there is a 180° shift in the way that water behaves in the different hemispheres, it seems logical and essential to take this into consideration.

Also, the spin of the Earth causes the winds in the Northern hemisphere to curve to the right and, in the Southern hemisphere, to curve to the left. This is called the Coriolis effect.

As a result of this, in the Northern hemisphere, winds blow clockwise around an area of high pressure and anti-clockwise around an area of low pressure. This is exactly reversed in the Southern hemisphere.

The seasons in the two hemispheres are the exact opposite of each other. Of course it makes a difference, in terms of survival, whether you are born in winter or summer, spring or autumn. The forces of nature are far more potent than we are. We make the adaptation to nature. It influences our development.

Although many leading feng shui authorities do not agree about this, the logic for dealing with Kua numbers, respecting the difference in the 2 hemispheres of our planet, would seem to be both overwhelming and compelling.

Added to this, my experience with Southern hemisphere born clients has shown that their results improve noticeably, when they use their Kua numbers calculated for the Southern hemisphere.

HOW TO FIND YOUR KUA NUMBER

For Men born in the Northern hemisphere

If you were born before the 4th February, start by subtracting 1 from your year of birth. Add all the digits of this year together. If necessary, reduce this number to a single digit. Then take this number and subtract it from 11. This is your Kua number (and also your 9 Star Ki number).

If you were born after the 4th February, simply add all the digits of your year of birth together, and reduce this number to a single digit, if necessary, by adding the two numbers together. Then subtract this number from 11. This is your Kua number (and also your 9 Star Ki number).

To re-cap:

1. Subtract 1 from your year of birth if born BEFORE February 4th or 5th.

   If you were born AFTER 4th or 5th of February, take your year of birth only.

2. Now add all the digits of your year of birth together.

3. Reduce this number, if it is more than a single digit, to a single digit, by adding the numbers together.

   e.g. 1978 becomes:

   $1 + 9 + 7 + 8 = 25$

   Reduce 25 to a single digit:

   $2 + 5 = 7$

4. Subtract this single digit number from 11. The resulting number is your Kua number.

$11 - 7 = 4$

Therefore, the Kua number is 4

NB If this number is 5, then your Kua number becomes 2.

Example 1

Birth date is BEFORE 4th February

Birth date 12th January 1978

Step 1	$1978 - 1$	=	1977
Step 2	$1 + 9 + 7 + 7$	=	24
Step 3	$2 + 4$	=	6
Step 4	$11 - 6$	=	5 the exception!

Therefore, the Kua number is 2

Example 2

Birth date is AFTER 4th February

Birth date 31st September 1975

Step 1	$1 + 9 + 7 + 5$	=	22
Step 3	$2 + 2$	=	4
Step 4	$11 - 4$	=	7

Therefore, the Kua number is 7

Also, if you are a man born in the Northern hemisphere this number will be the same as your 9 Star Ki number.

Process for Men born in the Southern hemisphere, i.e. below the equator:

1. If you were born after the 7th or 8th of August, subtract 5 from your year of birth.

2. If you were born before the 7th or 8th August, subtract 6 from your year of birth.

3. Repeat steps 3 and 4 as for a man born in the Northern hemisphere (see below).

Reduce this number, if it is more than a single digit, to a single digit, by adding the numbers together.

e.g. 1966 becomes:

1 + 9 + 6 + 6 = 22

Reduce 22 to a single digit:

2 + 2 = 4

Subtract this single digit number from 11.

The resulting number is your Kua number.

11 − 4 = 7

Therefore, the Kua number is 7.

If this number is 5, your Kua number becomes 2.

Example 1

Birth date is AFTER 7th/8th August

Birth date 25th October 1971

Step 1	1971 − 5	=	1966
Step 2	1 + 9 + 6 + 6	=	22
Step 3	2 + 2	=	4
Step 4	11 − 4	=	7

Therefore, the Kua number is 7

Example 2

Birth date is BEFORE 7th/8th August

Birth date 17th May 1969

Step 1	1969 − 6	=	1963
Step 2	1 + 9 + 6 + 3	=	19
Step 3	1 + 9	=	10
	Reduce to a single digit		
	1 + 0	=	1
Step 4	11 − 1	=	10
	Reduce to a single digit		
	1 + 0	=	1

Therefore, the Kua number is 1

Process for Women born in the Northern hemisphere, i.e. above the equator:

1. Subtract 1 from your year of birth if you were born BEFORE 4th or 5th February.

2. Take this adjusted year and add all the digits together. If this number is 9 or less, consider it to be the remainder, as in step 3 of this process.

3. Divide this number by 9. If there is no remainder, the remainder is 0.

4. Add 4 to this remainder and this gives you your Kua number.
   (If this gives you a number with 2 digits, reduce this to a single digit by adding them together, e.g. for 11, 1 + 1 = 2)

   NB If this number is 5, your Kua number becomes 8.

Example 1

Birth date 3rd January 1983

Step 1	1983 − 1	=	1982	
Step 2	1 + 9 + 8 + 2	=	20	
Step 3	20 ÷ 9	=	2	with a remainder of 2
Step 4	4 + 2	=	6	

Therefore, the Kua number is 6.

Example 2

Birth date 25th August 1990

Step 1	Birth date after 4th February, therefore use 1990			
	1 + 9 + 9 + 0	=	19	
Step 2	19 ÷ 9	=	2	with a remainder of 1
Step 3	4 + 1	=	5	the exception!

Therefore, the Kua number is 8.

Example 3

Birth date 3rd June 1980

Step 1	$1 + 9 + 8 + 0$	$=$	18	
Step 2	$18 \div 9$	$=$	2	with no remainder
Therefore remainder		$=$	0	
Step 3	$4 + 0$	$=$	4	

Therefore, the Kua number is 4

Process for Women born in the Southern hemisphere, i.e. below the equator:

1. If you were born BEFORE the 7th or 8th of August, subtract 1 from your year of birth. Otherwise use your year of birth.

2. Take this adjusted year, and add all the digits together:

Example for a date before 7th or 8th August 1970

$1970 - 1 = 1969$

$1969 = 1 + 9 + 6 + 9 = 25$

If this number is 9 or less, consider it to be the remainder, as in step 3.

3. Divide this number by 9

$25 \div 9 = 2$ with a remainder of 7

If there is no remainder, the remainder is 0.

4. Add 8 to this remainder and this gives you your Kua number.

$8 + 7 = 15$

Reduce this to a single digit, if necessary, by adding the numbers together

$1 + 5 = 6$

Therefore, the Kua number is 6
(NB If this number is 5, your Kua number becomes 8)

Example 1

Birth date 25th July 1971

Step 1	1971 − 1	=	1970	
Step 2	1 + 9 + 7 + 0	=	17	
Step 2	17 ÷ 9	=	1	with a remainder of 8
Step 3	8 + 8	=	16	
Step 4	1 + 6	=	7	

Therefore, the Kua number is 7

Example 2

Birth date 19th September 2001

Step 1	Birth date after 7th/8th August therefore use 2001			
	2 + 0 + 0 + 1	=	3	
Step 2	3 ÷ 9	=	0	with a remainder of 3
Step 3	8 + 3	=	11	
Step 4	1 + 1	=	2	

Therefore, the Kua number is 2

NB

If you are one of the people born around the time of the Chinese New Year in the Northern hemisphere, i.e. middle January to early February, OR late July to early August in the Southern hemisphere, you may want to check some of the websites which offer a more precise calculation of your Kua number.

Please bear in mind that the Chinese New Year is normally on the date of the New Moon around the end of January and beginning of February.

It can be as late as the 18th February, as it was in the year 2007.

Please note, that if you are in the Southern hemisphere and Chinese New Year occurs late, it will also be later in August for you. Look about 6 months ahead.

You can check this in any diary which shows the New Moon times.

GOOD DIRECTIONS FOR KUA NUMBERS

Kua Number	Breath of Prosperity	Heavenly Doctor	Relationships	Clarity
1	SE	E	S	N
2	NE	W	NW	SW
3	S	N	SE	E
4	N	S	E	SE
6	W	NE	SW	NW
7	NW	SW	NE	W
8	SW	NW	W	NE
9	E	SE	N	S

The enhancement for both the **'Breath of Prosperity'** and the **'Clarity'** directions is to add the element of **Water**.

This can be in the form of water itself, or any other form of liquid, especially precious liquids such as oil, wine, champagne and perfume.

Also using the colors blue and black in this area for decorations and soft furnishings acts as an enhancement.

The enhancement for the **'Heavenly Doctor'** direction is to add the element of **Fire**. Please note this direction also relates to **'Good Health'**. For further information regarding health, please see Chapter 5.

The safest and least expensive way of emphasizing the **Fire** element is by leaving on an electric light for 3 hours a day in the relevant compass sector.

Another way to enhance this area is to light candles here.

You can also use red or orange decorations, soft furnishings and anything that can be considered flame colored.

The feng shui cure for the **'Relationships'** area is to add the element of **Earth**. This is best achieved by adding semi-precious stones to this area. Particularly useful for romance is rose quartz. Amethyst is also very useful, especially around computers.

Generally speaking, it is best to keep clear quartz crystal away from areas frequently used by small children or young adults below the age of 13.

The reason for this is that clear quartz acts as both a transmitter and a receiver. As children and young adolescents do not have stable energy patterns, anything that emphasizes these imbalances will tend to throw them off center even more. Best avoided!

Even for adults, clear quartz needs to be washed in cold running water at least once a week, and every month or so, left out in sunlight for a few hours, to purify it energetically.

Certainly, if you have an argument, and there is clear quartz in the room, it needs to be washed as soon as possible, so that the energy of the argument is dispersed rather than held.

HOW CAN YOU USE THESE DIRECTIONS TO BEST EFFECT?

The odds are, you may already be doing so! Successful sales people very frequently will find, when they check with a compass, that they face one of their good directions automatically when they pitch for new business.

You tap your good directions by sitting and facing them and when sleeping, having your head pointing towards one of them. Adding one of the relevant 5 elements to these compass sectors will also emphasize them.

EXCEPTIONS TO THE RULE

As well as the Shar Chi direction, there are usually 1 or 2 directions each year that are best avoided, no matter what your Kua number. In other words, these directions take precedence over everything for that particular year, and ideally everyone would avoid tapping them.

Here they are up to the year 2020.

2012	East South East	North
2013	South South East	West
2014	South only	
2015	South South West	East
2016	West South West	North
2017	West	West
2018	West North West	South
2019	North North West	East
2020	North	

Please note that each of these sectors is a 30° pie shape measured from the center of your home/office.

INAUSPICIOUS DIRECTIONS

Kua Number	Disaster/ Accidents	5 Ghosts	6 Curses	Killing Direction/Severed Fate
1	W	NE	NW	SW
2	E	SE	S	N
3	SW	NW	NE	W
4	NW	SW	W	NE
6	SE	E	N	S
7	N	S	SE	E
8	S	N	E	SE
9	NE	W	SW	NW

It may be useful for you to check the inauspicious directions if you have been dealing with ongoing, seemingly, intractable problems. Provided you follow the sequence of feng shui actions suggested earlier, you are unlikely to cause an imbalance that will over emphasize one of these sectors.

Only check these directions and sectors if you are dealing with long-standing and ongoing problems that do not appear to be responding to other feng shui corrections. **Always** do the basics first i.e.

- 'Changes for the Year'

- Clutter clearing

- Bathroom and man-hole cover corrections

- Balancing missing space

before you tackle any of these inauspicious directions.

IF I LIVE IN A FAMILY, WHOSE KUA NUMBER DIRECTIONS DO I CHECK?

The question to ask yourself is 'Who is being affected by negative circumstances?'

You would then check their Kua number first. In any family situation, you would also always check the directions for the main bread winner.

In the case of a burglary, it may be that only the wife's jewelry is taken. This would mean that you check the wife's directions rather than the husband's. Often, the element ruling the stolen items also tells a tale.

One family gave away a substantial number of plants and shrubs as they re-organized their front and back gardens. A week or two later, the steering wheel of their car, with its stalk, was stolen to order for the air bag.

In feng shui terms, a lot of plant or **Wood** energy was removed. This element is controlled by the **Metal** element, which rules cars. A balance between the energies of **Wood** and **Metal** was preserved. What is interesting is that the steering wheel with its stalk actually looks like a cut flower! Flowers out of the garden and the 'flower' out of the car!

Also, in the 5 element cycle **Wood** is controlled by **Metal**. In order to balance less **Wood**, there was less **Metal**, i.e. less of the car. Cars are considered to be ruled by the **Metal** element for several reasons. As well as being made of metal, they move on 4 round wheels and create a circulation of people and things.

DISASTER/ACCIDENTS

Anything that causes worry or loss of money, as well as accidents relates to this sector. If your workshop or kitchen falls in this area, you need to be meticulous regarding safety. If you need to climb a ladder here, make sure the safety catch is on, and there is someone else with you in the house.

If you spill any water or liquids in this area, clean them up immediately and make sure that floors are dry.

Safety here includes checking wiring and cables.

Make sure that the area is clean, clear and uncluttered as well as being well lit.

This sector is ruled by the element of **Earth** and so its energy can be drained by using metal objects – something like a metal bowl would work. You can also control the **Earth** energy here using a living green plant.

Please refer back to Chapter 4, pages 50 – 51, for a reminder about the 5 element cycle.

5 GHOSTS

Ongoing disharmony at home, or at the office, or just a haunted atmosphere, can mean that you need to use a 'cure' in this sector. It also relates to injuries to one of your children, a burglary or a fire.

Placing a shrine here is an excellent 'cure'. There are many occasions when I have been to a clients' home, and found that one of their children has created a shrine in this area, acting as a positive balance point for the entire family.

As this area is ruled by the element of **Fire**, you can drain it by using the element of **Earth** e.g. porcelain and terracotta objects. You can control the energy of **Fire** by using the element of **Water**, especially water that has been exposed to sunlight for at least 3 hours.

6 CURSES

This relates to things that go wrong without being completely disastrous. This sector is usually concerned with legal problems. It can also be about accidents, financial loss, and illness. In the worst case scenario, it could even relate to death, either of an employee or relative.

This sector is ruled by the element of **Water**. This is, therefore, not a good area to place a fountain or a water feature. Instead use **Wood** energy, i.e. plants and green objects as well as candles, lights and red objects (**Fire** energy) to balance things out.

As **Fire** and **Water** are quite a strong clash of elements, only use the **Fire** element here with **Wood** energy.

The **Wood** energy drains the element of **Water** while the **Fire** element 'controls' the energy of **Water**. Again, please see the diagram about the 5 elements in Chapter 4, pages 50 – 51.

SEVERED FATE – ALSO CALLED THE 'KILLING' DIRECTION

Remember the principles of feng shui. This is definitely an area that you want to drain rather than enhance!

This direction relates to total ruin, possible loss of income, possible loss of a job, wife or husband, money and possibly death. Plans go array, health can also be affected.

This sector is ruled by the element of **Metal**. Good 'cures' would be **Water** element ruled things such as a fish tank or a small fountain. The **Water** element drains the **Metal**.

It is also possible to use **Fire** cures here as **Fire** 'controls' **Metal**. Examples of **Fire** element cures would be candles and red objects and also leaving the electric light on for a minimum of 3 hours a day.

GENERAL ADVICE

It is more important to emphasize your positive directions first before concerning yourself with the inauspicious ones.

9 times out of 10, if you follow the feng shui action sequences detailed in this book, you will get good results just from enhancing the positive directions.

The negative ones have been included for the sake of completeness.

BRINGING IT ALL TOGETHER

Shortcuts

Is this all a bit overwhelming?

Are you mentally going into overload, even considering where to begin?

You are not alone!

As they say, a journey of a thousand miles starts with just 1 step.

The most important thing is getting started.

Here are a few thoughts about the most practical ways to begin making the feng shui changes for your home.

Which area of your home/office do you like the least or actually dislike?

What are the simplest and easiest changes that you can make in this area, so that you at least like it OR dislike it less.

In which area of your home/office is there the most disorder?

What are the easiest things you can do to bring order into an area you dislike and/or which is disordered?

Are you challenged in 3 or more areas of your life at present? i.e. are you dealing with career problems, relationship problems and money problems? If this is the case, the 2 most important areas for you to space clear, bring order to and beautify are the **'Transformation'** area, sometimes called **'Knowledge'** and the **North East** sector of your home/office (mountain energy).

If your space is very cluttered, what works is to limit yourself to 7½ to 10 minutes a day of space clearing, accompanied by inspiring, rousing music. It is far better to do a little of this every day, rather than 3 hours on a Friday afternoon, and nothing for the next 3 months!

FOR THE THOROUGH AND METICULOUS

Checklist

NB The sequence of these feng shui adjustments is important. Often doing the first 3 items on this list is enough to create noticeable results.

There is a reason behind the sequence. Feng shui is about balance. You want positive change in your life, without causing major upsets at the same time.

1. Have you located the geometric center of your home and, if relevant, the plot of land in which your home sits?

   Please see Chapter 4.

2. Have you done the feng shui Changes for the Year?

   Please see Chapter 4.

3. Have you de-cluttered your home? Are all the corridors, hallways and interconnections between the rooms clear and uncluttered? Is your home clean and tidy?

   Please see Chapter 3.

4. Have you fixed or repaired any broken items and recycled or binned any that are irreparable?

5. Have you space cleared your home?

   Clear quartz crystals and semi precious stones, especially of the crystalline variety, hold very particular energies. Clear quartz, especially, needs to be washed in cold running water for several minutes every week, and every few weeks placed in sunlight, either in a garden or on a sunny window sill for several hours.

   Please see Chapter 3.

6. Have you corrected for any missing space on your floor plan?

    Please see Chapter 7.

7. Do you have stairs coming down directly opposite your front door? Have you corrected for this formation?

    Please see Chapter 7.

8. Does your bathroom fall in the geometric center of your home/office? If so, the correction is to mirror all the walls above waist height. Never reflect the toilet itself, and also never use mirrored tiles for this purpose, as this fragments your reflection, the equivalent of seeing yourself in pieces. Not a good look!

9. Is there a bathroom or toilet door directly opposite your front door? If so, ensure that you have done the bathroom corrections and, instead of a small convex mirror, place large distant view artwork on this door.

    If you are apartment/house hunting, this formation is usually best avoided, especially if this is the only bathroom in the property.

10. Have you done bathroom corrections? To recap:

    Keep the plugs in the sink, bath, and shower in

    Keep the lid of the toilet down

    Have as many green plants or objects in the area as possible – fake plants only if no other option

    Have some red objects in there unless the bathroom falls in the Shar Chi area for the year

    Place a small round convex mirror on the outside of the bathroom door at the throat height of the tallest person in the house.

11. Have you done the corrections for manhole covers? This involves placing a large heavy pot, nicely planted out, preferably with some flowers OR substituting the existing manhole covers for recessed ones planted out with something green and flowering, like camomile.

12. Have you ensured that you have no mirrors directly opposite each other?

13. With regard to stairs, are they closed at the back between the treads, and if not, can you find a way to close the back of the treads.

    Please see Chapter 7.

14. Have you identified your Kua number and your positive directions?

15. A room by room check:

Living room

Ensure that the corners of the room are lit, and that you have a large healthy vibrant green plant in the far left hand of the corner of the room, i.e. the **'Fortunate Blessings'** area of the living room.

Kitchen

Avoid having the cooker and the sink opposite each other. Please see Chapter 7.

Bathrooms

Keep the door to the bathroom shut, and do general bathroom corrections. Please see Chapter 8.

Bedrooms

Light the corners of the room.

Avoid placing your bed directly opposite the door.

Avoid mirrors in the bedroom if you are an adult. (For reasons please see Chapter 8).

Avoid any mirrors in the bedroom for small children and babies, and anyone who is suffering from insomnia.

Avoid underfloor heating in bedrooms generally, as this disturbs the electromagnetic flow of energy when you are sleeping, preventing you fully recharging your energies.

Avoid electrical equipment in your bedroom. Ensure any TVs or radio alarms are at least 6 feet (1.8 meters) away from your bed. This is for the same reason as avoiding underfloor heating, mentioned above.

Avoid sleeping over geopathic stress or vortex energy. Please see Chapter 5.

The loft / attic

This area represents the **'Heaven'** space and, therefore, relates to **'Helpful People'** and cash flow as well.

Ensure that what is here is really storage, and not just clutter that you have given up on!

The basement

This area is ruled by the energy of **Earth**, and is therefore concerned with relationships, and your unconscious mind.

Again, ensure that what is here is storage and not clutter. This is very important, especially if you are involved in any form of psychotherapy, either as a therapist yourself, or as a client.

The study

Avoid facing a wall if at all humanly possible, and also avoid having your back to the door.

If you must face a wall, hang some distant view artwork on it to symbolically open out the area.

If you must sit with your back to the door, have a very small mirror close to your computer or on the wall in front of you, so that if anyone comes in, the reflected light from this mirror will alert you.

Avoid having mirrors in offices, as this doubles the paperwork but not the profits!

Ensure that the far left hand corner and the **South East** of your study each have a light and a plant.

Finally, consider these additional tips:

Remember that there should be no wind chimes in any area that you are trying to enhance, unless, of course, it is the Shar Chi area for the year.

If you must have a mirror in your bedroom, hang it on the inside of your cupboard door, always assuming that this is not in the Shar Chi area for the year.

A dressing table mirror in your bedroom can be covered when not in use – again provided that it does not fall in the Shar Chi area for the year.

A LITTLE REMINDER

+   Flat mirrors, round glass faceted crystal balls and red objects add energy to an area.

–   Wind chimes and convex mirrors disperse energy in an area.

MIRRORS IN GENERAL

Avoid mirrors directly opposite one another as this creates a situation where it is seems to be impossible to break out of existing circumstances. This is called 'war of the mirrors'.

A mirror should reflect the head and shoulders of every adult member of the household. If it is technically beheading someone, it needs to be hung lower on the wall.

Mirrored tiles are best avoided as they split a person's image into fragments. The goal of feng shui is towards the integration of your total being.

A mirror magnifies what is opposite it, and what is on the wall behind it, even though it is in another room. If you reflect a blank wall you are multiplying nothing:

$$0 \times 0 = 0!$$

i.e. nothing multiplied by nothing equals more of nothing. Ensure that your mirrors reflect beauty, and the circumstances that you wish to draw into your life.

Convex mirrors act as deflectors. This is why a small convex mirror is ideal on the outside of a bathroom door because it deflects the energy of this room.

The reason for having the mirror at the throat height of the tallest person in the household is so that it does not deflect energy at the level of anyone's solar plexus or below.

This can cause members of the household to experience nausea and stomach upsets, as the bathroom energy is being directed to their lower chakras, which are the energy centers relating to digestion.

THE LAST RESORT…

In the unlikely event, that having done all this, no change is forthcoming, ensure that there are no feng shui 'cures' near the center of your home, and hang a single round glass faceted crystal ball in this area.

Please note that a small round glass faceted crystal ball, 1½ inches (2 – 3 cms) in diameter, is usually sufficient for most purposes. A round glass faceted crystal ball the size of a tennis or cricket ball is more suited to a large dining hall for several hundred people, i.e. as found in a stately home or hotel.

CONCLUSION

The purpose of feng shui is to increase the balance and harmony in your life generally, and to encourage an enjoyable, interesting, on-going relationship with that most important of all places, your home.

May everyone who reads this book have **'Fortunate Blessings'** – Health, Wealth and Happiness.

Jargon Buster

Additional Space	extra space on a floor plan which increases the square or rectangle by less than a third on each of its sides.
Ancestors	family going back beyond your grandparent's generation.
Bagua	an 8 sided figure where each side represents 1 of the 8 manifestations of life according to Taoist philosophy. It is used as a template and placed over the space being evaluated.
Cash flow	money that comes in every month or every week to pay bills, i.e. the gas, electricity, rent or mortgage and food.
Chakra	one of the 7 main energy centers in the human body.
Changes for the Year	feng shui adjustments for the particular Chinese New Year, which involve dispersing energy in the relevant compass sector. This always involves removing mirrors, red objects and round glass faceted crystal balls.
Chi	energy or life force.
Chinese New Year	always on a New Moon anywhere between late January and the middle of February. It is based on lunar cycles.
Control Cycle	flow of energy between the 5 elements which can be drawn in the shape of a pentagon, showing which element has control over, or destroys the next one in the sequence.
Coriolis Effect	The deflection of winds to the right in the Northern hemisphere and to the left in the Southern hemisphere due to the Earth's rotation.

Corrections	feng shui adjustments to balance the energy of a room or space.
Counter Measure	correction to minimize the effects of a move in an unfavorable direction.
Creative Cycle	flow of energy between the 5 elements which can be drawn in the shape of a circle showing which element nourishes the next one in the cycle.
Crystals	a) round glass faceted crystal balls. This refers to transparent glass balls with facets cut into them. They throw rainbows when hit by light.
	b) precious or semi-precious stone or mineral rock.
Cure	addition of any item of decoration or furniture, or elemental quality, deliberately placed to influence the energy in a room or space.
Destiny	preordained fate, a predetermined course of events.
Direction-ology	study of an individual's 9 Star Ki numbers to find good directions for travel, holidays and home/office moves and counter-measures for unfavorable directions
Directions	1 of the 8 major compass directions, i.e. North, South, East, West, North East, North West, South East, South West.
Dowsing	also known as 'Divining', is a technique using rods (or sometimes a forked branch or a pendulum) to detect the location of hidden objects or energies.
Earth Energy	considered female and Yin. The energy of home and centeredness. To do with all relationships, especially romantic ones.

East Life	personal description relating to a person's good directions when they are East, South East, North and South, i.e. an East Life person as opposed to a West Life person.
Eight (8) Directions	the 8 major compass directions, North, South, East, West, North East, North West, South East, South West.
Elders	area of the Bagua relating to living family and ancestors, the older generation and the compass sector East.
Element	1 of the 5 basic components of life on this planet in Taoist philosophy i.e. Earth, Metal, Water, Wood and Fire.
Energy	form of vitality and/or life. An expression of the life force.
Fate	power predetermining events from eternity.
Feng Shui (wind/water)	the art of balancing the energies and elements within a space to attract harmony and support particular life outcomes for the users of the space.
Fortunate Blessings	large sums of money, lottery winnings, winnings in general (Windfall Profits) especially when relating to large items such as houses or cars, extreme good fortune such as gaining large contracts, also the realization of a heart's desire.
Geopathic Stress	naturally occurring variation of the Earth's energy to which human beings react negatively. This energy may be responsible for health problems for people sleeping or working in areas affected by it.
Guardian Spirit	in many native traditions and some religions, each home is considered to have an angel or spirit presence whose responsibility it is to act as a caretaker for the space and its inhabitants.

Heaven Chi	considered to be male or Yang. Positive spirit energy which influences Earth and all its life forms.
Helpful People	an area of the Bagua that relates to anyone who renders you assistance, paid or unpaid. It may be that your plumber is more of a helpful person than your friend in certain circumstances! This area of the Bagua also relates to travel, Heaven energy and cash flow.
I Ching	translates into English as The Book of Changes and is sometimes translated as 'easy change'. The idea is that the only constant in life is change. The purpose of this oracle is to give advice to those who enquire of it so that these changes are easy.
Illumination	also known as 'Fame'. This is an area of the Bagua that relates to sudden enlightenment – the 'ah ha' moment we get when the penny suddenly drops. It also relates to actual fame and your reputation. It can be considered to be the Universe/God/The Source's communication with you. In the compass school of feng shui this is linked to the South.
Installation	all 5 elements present at once in a glass bowl. This consists of a glass bowl containing the following:

a clear or cut crystal glass bowl with a layer of semi-precious stones on the bottom	EARTH
a layer of coins on top of them	METAL
covered by water exposed to sunlight for 3 hours	WATER

with petals or floating flowers on top of the water	WOOD
with a floating candle or tea light lit for 3 hours a day	FIRE

Karma	the principle of cause and effect determining a person's life situation because of their actions or inactions.
Kidney Energy	The energy of the kidney meridian of the body, which in acupuncture terms, relates to the element of Water. This energy is also to do with reproduction and is the carrier of ancestral energy from one generation to the next. It also holds the body's reserve of energy.
Knowledge/ Transforma- tion	this area of the Bagua relates to learning and academic knowledge, as well as transformation in one's life and circumstances. Also known as 'Mountain' symbolizing the wise man's retreat to the mountains to reflect.
	It is about a person's relationship with the Universe/God/ The Source.
	It also relates to the North East in the compass school of feng shui.
Kua Number	derived from the Chinese year of your birth, depending on whether you are male or female, and also whether you were born in the Northern or Southern hemisphere.
	For each Kua number there are 4 good directions and 4 negative directions.
	NB there is no Kua number 5. If your calculations result in number 5, you are assigned Kua number 2 if you are a man, and Kua number 8 if you are a woman.

Magnetic North	the direction to which the red end of a compass needle always points. The Earth's magnetic field is inclined at about 11 degrees from its central axis of rotation. Because of this the Earth's magnetic pole does not correspond to the geographic North pole.
	Also, because the center of the Earth is molten, its magnetic field is always shifting slightly. For this reason, magnetic North can differ from true North by approximately 10 degrees or more.
Missing Space	a gap or space in a floor plan of a building so that it is not an even square or rectangle. At least one of its sides is more than one third of the building line.
Mountain Energy	area of the Bagua to do with Transformation/Knowledge and the North East sector of the compass. Also to do with the use of heavy solid objects, not easily moved, to add stability to an area.
Moving	
with the energy	moving in a compass direction which is favorable, according a person's 9 Star Ki number for the year.
against the energy	moving in a compass direction which is unfavorable, according to a person's 9 Star Ki number for the year.
Nine Star Ki (9 Star Ki)	a system of numerology based on the 5 elements, which also offers guidance on directions for travel.
Northern Hemisphere	all of planet Earth above the equator.
Numerology	the study of numbers relating to a person's date of birth and their influence on the person's life.

Predecessor Chi	the energy of a home or office that relates to its previous occupants.
Provenance	the history of an object, especially an antique.

....

Schumann Waves	the steady pulse of 7.83Hz within the ionosphere created by the approximately 9 million lightning strikes a day that hit our planet. It is also the dominant brainwave frequency of all mammals.
Shar Chi	negative energy as in unhelpful, pessimistic and draining.
Southern Hemisphere	all of planet Earth below the equator.
Space Clearing	using any or all of the Western elements of Earth, Air, Fire and/or Water

i.e. salt	– EARTH
smudging with sage smoke	– AIR and FIRE
bell ringing, music & chanting	– AIR
sprinkling with holy water or water that you have blessed	– WATER
lighting candles	– FIRE

or any of the 5 elements, Earth, Metal, Water, Wood and Fire

EARTH	– as above
METAL	– bell ringing
WATER	– as above
WOOD	– sprinkling petals and/ or flower essences
FIRE	– as above

to purify the energy of a room, a house or an outdoor space, and establish a positive background vibration of harmony and love.

Tai Chi	center of the Bagua relating to health. Translates as 'energy of peace'.
Taoism	the great way or natural laws of the Universe within which everything exists, according to the Chinese teachings of Lao-tzu.
True North	the geographic North pole where all longitude lines meet at the top of the Earth. All maps are drawn with true North directly at the top.
Vortex	a type of whirling, spiralling energy.
Yang	absolute masculine energy, having the qualities of brightness, heat, expansion and electrical positivity. Relates by expanding outwards, away from itself.
Yin	absolute feminine energy, having the qualities of darkness, cold, contraction and electrical negativity. Relates by pulling energy inwards, towards itself.
Zen	a Japanese form of Buddhism originating in 12th century China, advocating contemplation of one's essential nature to the exclusion of all else, as the only way of achieving enlightenment.
3 Gate Method of Chi	type of feng shui which lays the 8 sided Bagua over a floor plan, where the main entrance to the main property must fall in 'Knowledge/Transformation', 'Career' or 'Heaven/Helpful People'.
5 Elements	the Chinese consider that there are 5 basic elements. These are: Earth, Metal, Water, Wood and Fire.

Index